THE DAY WAR BROKE OUT
Stories of Life in a Village at War

The Sanderling—'C' Flight Heavy Conversion Unit, Riccall, 1944. Standing ninth from the left L.A.C. 'Bertie' Brickell now Managing Director of the firm who produced the book!

THE DAY WAR BROKE OUT
Stories of Life in a Village at War

John Booth

1984
Cambridge House Books
Westbury, Wiltshire

FIRST EDITION
Limited to 3,000 copies
with a Foreword by
Stan Richards
and an introduction by
Jimmy Wright OBE., DFC
on behalf of
ST. DUNSTAN'S
for men and women blinded on
War Service.

ISBN 0 906853 04 4

Printed in Great Britain
by
The Blackmore Press
Shaftesbury, Dorset.

In memory of
Roy Haslam

"Count your blessings and
Do not worry about growing old —
For old age is a privilege
Denied to many!"

Anon

The Tales

Line drawings by 'Les' Davison

Foreword

When I was asked to record some of these stories for Hospital Radio and for the blind, I realised that John was a fellow Yorkshireman of the worst kind ... he'd emigrated!

Living in the West Country for many years may be a lovely experience, but nothing can replace the 'BROAD ACRES' of your native county, and, may I add in John's case, never will.

I've sat in the 'Anchor' and the 'Ferry Inn' and I've stood on the splendid bridge at Cawood (which is more than poor Wolsey ever could).

This little book is full of delightful stories of a Yorkshire village which hasn't changed all that much in the last fifty years.

It is published in support of a very worthy cause, so please buy it — if you borrow it, your next door neighbour could be upset — because he *did* buy it!

Keep smiling,
STAN RICHARDS.

Introduction

by Jimmy Wright OBE, DFC

on behalf of St. Dunstan's

I am particularly pleased to be given the opportunity to commend to you this book, as John Booth has dedicated it to his friend the late Roy Haslam, a fellow member of the Guinea Pig Club, and a St. Dunstaner. Roy Haslam and I were patients of Sir Archibald McIndoe, at the Queen Victoria Hospital, East Grinstead, and Roy was one of four members of the Guinea Pig Club who lost their sight.

We are delighted that John intends to donate the proceeds of his book to St. Dunstan's, the charity that cares for blinded Service men and women, and I wish him every success.

I know you will enjoy reading these wonderfully funny tales of a Yorkshire tyke.

Jimmy Wright   7th August 1984

LOCATION MAP

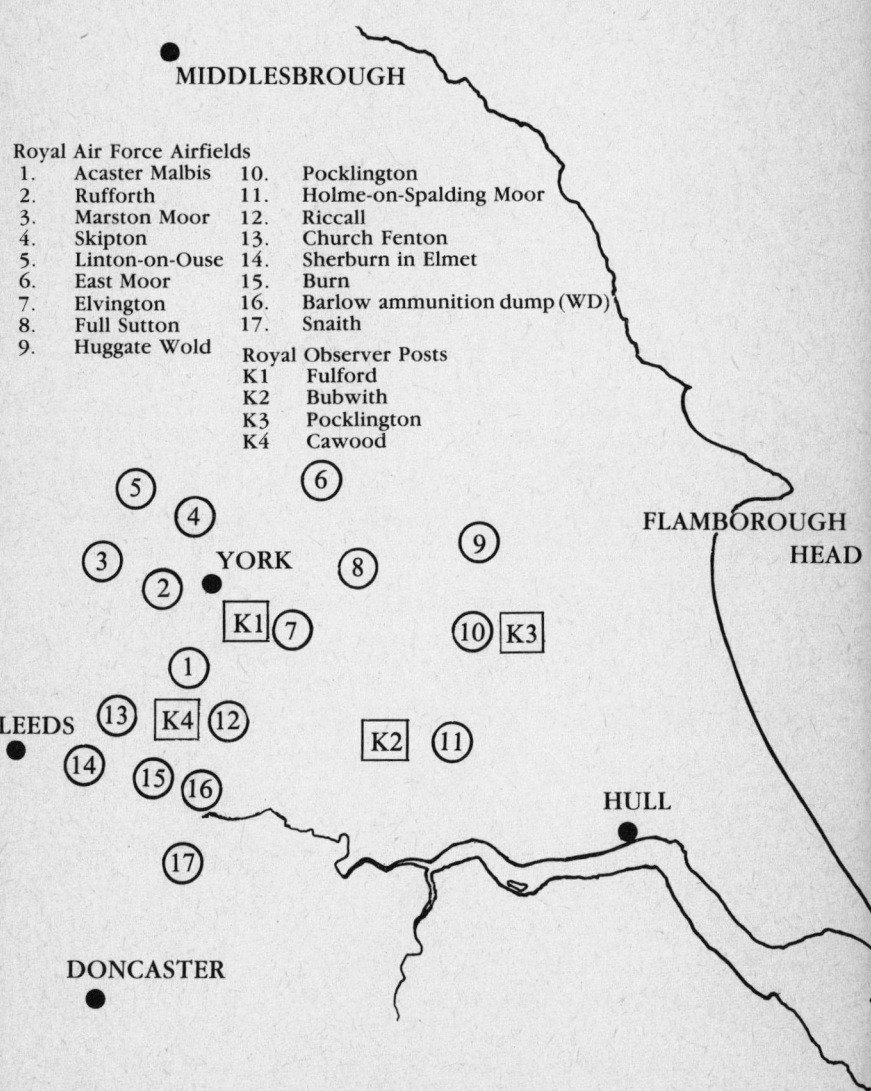

MIDDLESBROUGH

Royal Air Force Airfields
1.   Acaster Malbis   10.   Pocklington
2.   Rufforth   11.   Holme-on-Spalding Moor
3.   Marston Moor   12.   Riccall
4.   Skipton   13.   Church Fenton
5.   Linton-on-Ouse   14.   Sherburn in Elmet
6.   East Moor   15.   Burn
7.   Elvington   16.   Barlow ammunition dump (WD)
8.   Full Sutton   17.   Snaith
9.   Huggate Wold

Royal Observer Posts
K1   Fulford
K2   Bubwith
K3   Pocklington
K4   Cawood

FLAMBOROUGH
HEAD

YORK

LEEDS

HULL

DONCASTER

SHEFFIELD

Prelude

Long before the war a Sunday family walk to nearby Kelfield was greeted by great excitement in the village, the sky being shrouded with the white smoke of a nearby farm fire. A plea to father that we seek out the fire engine appeared to go unnoticed until we came to the brickyard pond and there she was. A bright red Merryweather fire engine tended by a giant in a brass helmet and wearing the largest pair of knee-boots that I had ever seen.

The great man appeared to be on friendly terms with father and soon a surprised and delighted ten-year-old was hoisted aboard the mighty throbbing engine and allowed to sit in the driver's seat. The memorable visit ended with 2nd Officer Moate placing his shiny helmet on my head. Yes, no doubt about it — when I grew up, I would be a fireman!

When you are young and the country is at war, employment prospects in this rural part of Yorkshire were somehow limited and lacking in excitement. Certainly there was evidence of moves that were afoot to turn the Plain of York into a vast military arsenal, and village names like Driffield, Pocklington, Burn and Rufforth took on a new meaning as their heavy bombers roared off into the night skies with deadly cargoes.

Our village was bursting with troops at this time, and day and night there was the constant roar of aircraft overhead as Church Fenton's Blenheims, Spitfires and Mosquitoes patrolled the skies; once causing a wayward German bomber to jettison its load, a stick of bombs that would have fallen right across the village had they been released moments later.

Our first tale opens on the 3rd of September 1939 with a story somewhat reminiscent of Rob Wilton's famous monologue and illustrates how an early wartime measure affected the lives of youngsters living in a Yorkshire village as yet untouched by war.

The day War broke out! or Fireworks at the Bridge

The village of Cawood nestles quietly on the old West Riding bank of Yorkshire's River Ouse and displays a present day tranquillity that belies its turbulent past, for here in their turn came Roman, Saxon, Dane and Norman, all anxious to fill their bellies with the spoils of war.

Centuries later, the disgraced Cardinal Wolsey came to Cawood to escape the wrath of an ungrateful monarch, as also did the proud Duke of Newcastle at the head of a great Northern Royalist Army that was later to die at Marston Moor when King gave way to Commonwealth and ended Civil War.

Today's visitor to Cawood will doubtless see the fine 13th Century Parish Church and the old Castle Gatehouse, all that now remains of a once proud Palace, and above, the very Courtroom where poor Wolsey was arrested and charged with treason for having served his King too well!

Of somewhat more recent date, is Cawood's splendid Bridge; a masterpiece of late Victorian engineering whose operation as a swing bridge is achieved simply by turning a handle. In a matter of minutes, this action will revolve a hundred-yard section of the roadway weighing several hundred tons into the 'open' position, allowing large vessels to navigate the river from the Humber Estuary, as far as the City of York some ten miles upstream.

In 1939 our family had been at the Bridge for longer than most people could remember, the post of Bridgemaster apparently passing by natural succession from

'Father took a great pride in his bridge . . .'

grandfather to eldest son and upon his death, to father, the youngest and only surviving son.

Father took a great pride in his bridge and in the smart dark blue uniform and peaked cap bearing the word 'Bridgemaster' in silver braid. Together with his assistant George, the various tasks of looking after the bridge went ahead with the precision of a well-oiled watch. It was frequently opened for the passage of river traffic and the navigation lights that were positioned on either buttress had to be cleaned, trimmed and re-filled each day. Tide times and river heights were recorded with meticulous care in father's fine copper-plate hand in a large log-book which also contained the names and numbers of all commercial shipping passing through the bridge.

Each week, this information would be entered on separate sheets and the details sent to the County Hall Mandarins at Wakefield, who doubtless took great comfort from the fact that the 'Brunton' the 'Bishopthorpe' the 'Ouse' and the 'Alice of York', in company with many more — had all passed safely through Cawood Bridge together with the various cargoes. Navigating the bridge was not without its hazards; sometimes an error of judgement, or sheer bad luck on the part of a tillerman on one of the following barges, would result in the heavy fast-moving vessel striking a bridge buttress and there would be a grinding crash that usually tore giant splinters from the woodwork and left father dancing with rage on the bridge above.

My favourite was the 'Ouse', a fast-moving river tug with a huge funnel that belched volumes of black smoke when she was in a hurry. Father always seemed to know when she wanted the bridge, for at other times she would bear down upon us at high speed and at the last moment, her great hinged funnel would be lowered and she would pass smoothly beneath the bridge, accompanied by a spin of her wheel and a friendly wave and a smile from her skipper.

The 'nerve centre' of this far flung outpost of the West Riding County Council Roads and Bridges Department (for across the river lay the East Riding) was the 'cabin' which enjoyed the proportions and appearance of a small chicken house. It had been conveniently built in the centre of the bridge and so obstructed the nearside roadway that vehicles leaving for the East Riding had to give way to oncoming traffic. Its strategic location was a factor that had not escaped the eagle eye of Police Constable Hutton, or his somewhat less flexible successor — P.C. Wilkes. In consequence, father was provided with endless lists of the registration numbers of stolen cars. As at that time there were less than five cars in our village, I remembered thinking that there must be a great many wealthy car owners elsewhere in the West Riding!

On Sunday the 3rd of September 1939, the normal routine at Bridge House was following its usual pattern until the announcement from father that the Prime Minister was to broadcast to the nation at 11 o'clock. This comment was made to my mother in my absence, for I was in my bedroom putting the finishing touches to a flying model of a Westland Lysander.

The first intimation this twelve-year-old had of the gravity of his position was when mother rushed in. 'Had

I collected the wireless accumulator from Mr. Todd's yesterday?' 'Well yes I had but, no I hadn't'. 'And what is that supposed to mean?' demanded mother, an air of menace in her voice. 'Well I went to collect it, but I was talking to Mr. Todd about the special accumulator he is trying to find for my cine projector and I forgot it'. 'For goodness sake go and get it before your father finds out'. 'Why can't I go later? I want to fix the bomb racks on my Lysander'. 'Your father wants to hear the Prime Minister on the wireless at eleven o'clock'. Events were now decidedly taking a serious turn, for father's wrath posed a far greater threat than anything Mr. Chamberlain might say, or for that matter Mr. Hitler either!

Mr. Todd's cycle and wireless shop was only fifty yards along the High Street from where we lived. I knew he was always in the shop on Sunday mornings and remember him as a tall, kindly man, much addicted to soldering, his bench often covered with the magical bits and pieces from the various wireless sets the villagers brought in for repair. I had also noticed that he sometimes seemed addicted to soldiering as well, for on Armistice Day each year at precisely 11 o'clock, he would stand quietly and bare-headed at the bus-stop near the Market Place, holding the flag of the local British Legion in a silent tribute to the dead of the Great War.

Mr. Todd's shop was an Aladdin's cave for me. It was filled with a marvellous jumble of bicycle pumps and lamps, Sturmey Archer Sprockets, tins of carbide, high tension batteries, and lots and lots of bicycle bulbs, all sitting in neat rows in cardboard trays. Surprisingly, father did not appear to share my views about Mr. Todd's window — he said it looked like the bottom of a parrot cage, and anyway, that man was a Bolshevik. I didn't know what a Bolshevik was, and father's efforts to enlighten me fell on rather stony ground. All I knew was that my Bolshevik friend was kind and clever, and I loved talking to him.

Father was clever too, of course; he had been a carpenter and joiner before he became Bridgemaster and kept lots of tools in a big black box under the stairs which he never opened. Mr. Todd had lots of tools, although they were usually spread about all over his bench

'. . . *and there would be a grinding crash that usually tore giant splinters from the woodwork . . .*'

and he used to spend a great deal of time trying to find a particular one that always seemed to be missing!

I handed Mr. Todd my fourpence and retrieved the precious accumulator — the problem now was to get it indoors without father seeing me. I need not have worried, for he was holding court outside his cabin on the bridge with P.C. Wilkes, the granite-featured guardian of local law and order. Safely indoors, I unscrewed the terminals on the run-down accumulator, quickly replacing it with the new one. I switched on the set and the 'Blue Spot' speaker replied from its large plywood baffle hanging on the living room wall. Bridge House was now ready to receive all that Mr. Chamberlain had to tell on this fateful day.

The church clock struck ten and I realized it would soon be time to join the two Archbishops of York who slumbered peacefully in the Parish Church of Cawood All Saints. Matins was at 10.30 and the Reverend John Baxter Unthank was blessed with a small, but loyal supporting cast of choir and congregation. At about this time on Sunday mornings, the Lupton's, uncle and nephew, would start ringing the church bells and for the best part of half an hour their peals would ring out across the waters of the river to the village beyond. On this particular Sunday morning, news of the Prime Minister's intended broadcast appeared to have had a serious effect on the numbers attending church. After a short address, during which the vicar outlined the gravity of the international situation to a congregation of six, including two choir-boys, there were prayers for peace and the service ended.

I reached home some few minutes later to find both my parents and young sister listening intently to the wireless — the Blue Spot speaker had not let me down. I was in time to hear Mr. Chamberlain say in a quiet, firm voice that an ultimatum demanding the immediate withdrawal of German troops from Poland had remained unanswered. 'I have to tell you that no such undertaking has been received' he said, 'and that consequently, this country is now at war with Germany'.

Several weeks later, war or no war, life in Cawood continued as before until the Sunday morning that Mr. Pollard, husband of our local post-mistress, arrived at Bridge House with a large sack on his back, looking very much like an out-of-season Father Christmas. A shake of his head in my direction, an understanding nod from father, and two heads came together in whispered conversation which culminated in a quiet 'All right Bert you carry on' from father. Bert carried on. Clutching his sack, he left the house and started to cross the bridge. Father resumed reading the Sunday paper and I walked through the living room en route for the outside closet! Once across the yard, so to speak, I left by the back gate and trotted smartly around the house and onto the bridge.

I was in time to see that Mr. Pollard had stopped halfway across and was fumbling with the string tied round the neck of his mysterious sack. Clearly, something was destined for the watery wastes below and obviously Mr. Pollard had thought it necessary to clear the disposal with father before proceeding. I paused and viewed the river in the opposite direction — better lean over the parapet and look uninterested. It worked! and Mr. Pollard renewed his attack on the sack with what seemed to me, feverish haste.

I speculated as to its contents. Perhaps their dog had died, or maybe he had been doing some decorating and it was a sackful of old wallpaper. That couldn't be I mused, for father was very particular about what people threw in his river! I edged nearer the scene of the crime and then, with a mighty flourish, Mr. Pollard held the sack aloft by its bottom corners — and the contents cascaded into the river.

I couldn't believe my eyes. Mr. Pollard, who always seemed to me to be a very reasonable person — had just tipped the best part of half a hundred weight of fireworks into the river! There was everything; jumping crackers, catherine wheels, roman candles, ha'penny demons and even rockets — the latter on giant sticks, now turning gently in the eddies below. They cost at least one and a tanner each I told myself — that was eighteen weeks' pocket money!

'Mr. Pollard, who always seemed to me to be a very reasonable person — had just tipped the best part of half a hundred weight of fireworks into the river!'

Two or three fireworks hit the hand-rail of the bridge and landed on the decking and I rushed across to save them but Mr. Pollard was too quick for me. I just had time to read the maker's name 'Brock's' before he scooped them up and they joined the remainder in the river below. Without a word, Mr. Pollard folded up his sack and walked quickly away and I watched the bobbing procession as it picked up speed in the river below and disappeared downstream in the direction of the church.

The previous year, our Bonfire Night had been a milestone in the history of the village. Weeks before the event, local farmers had trekked to the site in Rythergate with their horses and carts depositing loads of suitable refuse for the bonfire. Ralph Lund, Cubmaster and village handyman, had made a giant guy. He sat comfortably on a large barrel of gunpowder in his black flowing cloak and tall hat, a torch grasped in his right hand. Ralph's handcart was pressed into service and with ropes attached fore and aft, the cubpack paraded Mr. Fawkes around the village, headed by the drum and bugle band of the 1st Cawood Boy Scouts. At 7 pm precisely, Miss Unthank, President of the Women's Institute, lit the bonfire, her ladies moving amongst the large crowd of villagers who had assembled, selling home-made toffee apples, brandy snaps and parkin.

With last year's bonfire very much in mind, I walked sadly to the house, remembering that I had heard father say that people do things in war that they would never dream of doing in peacetime.

I remarked that I had just seen Mr. Pollard acting very strangely — did he think that the war was to blame? 'Yes, he was afraid it was; the Government had just issued orders that all pyrotechnics must be destroyed and fireworks were included in the order'.

'But if we have no fireworks, what about the fifth of November and the bonfire' I demanded. 'There won't be any more of that kind of thing until the war's over, by which time you will have probably seen all the fireworks you are ever likely to want to see', said father philosophically and indicated that the interview was over and turned his attention to the Sunday newspaper.

They shall not Pass

After ten months of war, which included the victorious battle of the River Plate, many pointless leaflet 'raids' on Germany by the Whitley bombers from Driffield and Linton-on-Ouse and the tragedy and miracle of Dunkirk, the strategic role of Cawood Bridge in the event of invasion (which now seemed imminent) was becoming a matter of concern to father. The bridge was a vital link between the coast and the West Riding. A German landing in the north-east would place the River Ouse and its bridges directly in the path of an attack on the industrial cities of Yorkshire and the Midlands.

The Bridgemaster wrote to County Hall expressing his fears and suggested that an approach be made to the appropriate authorities regarding suitable defences for the bridge. His request received sympathetic consideration from the County Hall Mandarins. 'You can rest assured that contingency plans are in hand in the event of such a threat developing' wrote the County Surveyor encouragingly in his reply.

'They don't give a damn' said father later, in an attempt to share some of his concern with his assistant. 'Don't worry Sid', said George, 'If the "Jerries" do come we can always send 'em round by Selby Toll Bridge. They don't care who they let over so long as they pay!'

George received a withering look at this attempt to introduce a little humour into what father considered was a serious situation. Needless to say, when the 'master plan' for the defence of Cawood Bridge was conceived, George was excluded from the deliberations.

The bridge 'defence committee' held its first meeting some days later in the cabin with the Bridgemaster 'in the

'If the "Jerries" do come we can always send 'em round by Selby Toll Bridge.'

chair' or, to be more precise, on the cabin stool! The three-man committee included Police Constable Wilkes representing the County Constabulary and Ralph Lund, cubmaster and village handyman, now deputising for George and father on their rest-days. Ralph, like father, brought a wealth of military experience to the task from an earlier encounter with this same enemy some twenty years previously.

'The problem is quite straightforward', explained father. 'How do we stop the "Jerries" using the bridge without the aid of explosives which we don't have?' 'We could swing it, Sid' Ralph said hopefully, the remark almost sounding as if it was meant to have musical overtones. 'And what's to stop them getting a bloody boat or swimming out and shutting it again?' demanded father heatedly. 'Well, what do you suggest Sid?' asked P.C. Wilkes easily, rising to his feet as his eagle eye caught sight of me eavesdropping outside the cabin door. I beat a hasty retreat in the direction of Bridge House. Now I would never know how father proposed to foil the Germans!

At this point readers who may happen to be retired military gentlemen, civil engineers, or for that matter anyone remotely interested in the strategic defence of Yorkshire's West Riding in the 1940's, may wish to leave us and proceed by whatever means they may have at their disposal to Cawood Bridge, there to ponder afresh the problem facing our gallant trio as to how best to deny its use to the Germans?

Those remaining will no doubt want to know something of the plans that were afoot to turn the bridge into the impregnable fortress it later became. It certainly made the enemy think twice about their proposed invasion of Yorkshire and it was rumoured at the time that they decided to go to Russia instead!

It is only now, nearly forty-five years later, that one of the best-kept secrets of the war can be revealed. The cabin on the bridge became an Armoury! At first there was little evidence of this change of role, apart from a large padlock fitted to the door and several trips by Wilf Storr, the village carpenter and wheelwright. Visitors to the cabin were now surprised to see two vintage World

War One 'Ross' rifles standing smartly to attention in a polished hardwood rack attached to the inside panelling. Hanging above were two regulation pattern steel helmets for use by the defenders.

For his part the third member of the bridge committee had already been issued with the necessary protective headgear, with the word 'Police' in white letters on a blue background. This led me to the belief that any invading Germans would have a due respect for the law and not shoot him!

The role of P.C. Wilkes was vital to the success of the defence strategy, father inclining to the view that in the event of enemy parachutists being dropped in the locality, he would be the first to know. In such an eventuality he would mount his cycle and pedal with all speed to the bridge with the fateful news, a most necessary step because at this time the bridge was without a telephone link with the outside world. This unfortunate omission was later to hold up the war for at least five hours and cause considerable distress and inconvenience to the officer-in-charge of one of His Majesty's armoured columns.

On hearing from the police and after due consultation the defenders would proceed to 'swing' the bridge, taking up their respective defensive positions in the Engine Room with their rifles. The Engine Room (or Drawing Room as father affectionately called it) was a sort of natural bunker which contained the mechanism for operating the bridge, whose metal cladding would provide the ideal defence against small-arms fire. These various preparations went ahead in great secrecy but certain natural 'gleanings' came my way for I was certain that father had not been provided with the rifles in order to go rabbit shooting!

I was now almost fourteen and able to swing the bridge without father's help as he was experiencing increasing difficulty with his breathing. According to the doctor this was the result of a liberal dose of mustard-gas in the 1914–18 war which had seriously damaged his bronchial tubes.

He had fared badly at the hands of the Germans, having been wounded three times, once almost fatally, when a stray bullet cut a deep groove in his forehead and resulted in a subsequent eyebrow growth that would have made Mr Dennis Healey green with envy! Both he and Ralph had much in common as old soldiers but neither was prepared to speak about his experiences in the previous war, except for a shared conviction that the only good Germans were dead ones.

I recollect sitting with him one evening in the cabin on the bridge just as the tide had turned as we waited for the far-away throb of boats returning downstream from York on their way back to the Humber. Over to the East the sky was alight with fires and the distant thud of falling bombs. Yes, father had been right about the fireworks he had mentioned in the early days of the war. 'Them's Flaming Onions!' he said, gesturing with his arm in the direction of a group of bright lights high in the sky over Hull. 'The "Jerries" are using them to see where to drop their bombs!' The cabin was warm and comfortable and I felt a reassurance from his presence that made the war seem far away. He didn't seem the least bit frightened but suddenly the glow from the slightly open door of the cabin's stove reflected on the metal of the newly installed rifles and brought me quickly back to reality.

'What will you do if the Germans come Dad.' I asked cautiously. 'I shall shoot 'em son, or as many as I can before they get me', he replied quietly. 'But surely you can't stop them capturing the bridge all on your own?' I demanded. He thought for a moment before replying and then continued. 'They may capture it son, but Ralph and I will make damn certain that they will never be able to make use of it. Providing we can swing it before they get here, we shall shelter in the Drawing Room and if the position looks hopeless we shall break the cast-iron cogs of the winding mechanism with my sledge-hammer and they will never be able to close it again.'

Of course! This explained the recent disappearance of the hammer from the coal-house; it was already in the Engine Room in readiness for any eventuality.

It also explained the repeated trips I had seen father and Ralph making to the Engine Room as they disappeared below-decks from time to time carrying various bits and pieces.

The air-raid siren began to wail its warning in anticipation of things to come. It always frightened me more than any of the action that sometimes followed. 'Come on lad, it's way past bedtime. Off you go back to the house or mother will be worried', said father. Mother did worry and I knew the drill. It was either under the stairs, or the dining-room table with my young sister, our heads encased in small galvanised baths at the sound of approaching aircraft. These would help to protect us in the event of flying glass or splinters insisted mother.

I noticed that the enemy aircraft seemed to have engines which made a different sound from the British ones, a sort of mmm-ah, mm-ah, mmm-ah. My other concern was the fact that they always seemed to pass right over our house! Dad had worked that out too. 'They fly along the coast from the south to the Humber Estuary, then use the major rivers to guide them inland', he commented with authority one morning at breakfast.

But Mother wasn't the only one who worried; so it seems did Mr. Goodson, Dad's boss from the County Roads and Bridges Department. He was sitting in the living room with father on my arrival from school a few weeks later.

'We appear to have a weight problem', said Mr. Goodson, casting a reflective glance in father's direction. Father eyed his waistline. 'No! No! not you Mr. Booth, the bridge!' said Mr. Goodson hastily. Father eyed him reproachfully. Nobody could say that Sid Booth was fat, at least not if they wished to survive the encounter. Mr. Goodson took a deep breath and continued. 'When Cawood Bridge was built there were no motor vehicles and we cannot blame the designer for failing to anticipate them', went on Mr. Goodson. Father nodded. Mr. Goodson looked relieved and continued. 'It is imperative that the six-ton limit for the bridge is strictly enforced, otherwise my engineers are convinced that one day a heavily laden lorry will end up floating down the river', he added with a certain relish. Once again father found himself nodding in agreement.

It was consequently ordained that the six-ton limit for Cawood Bridge would be strictly enforced 'come hell or highwater' as father put it. That apart, the large notices at either end of the bridge proclaimed it, Mr. H. R. Hepworth the County Surveyor endorsed it, and Mr. Goodson, his noble deputy, was now demanding it. Cawood Bridge would thus continue to survive intact and in majestic splendour until the end of the age; providing at all times ready access between East and West Ridings, without let or hindrance for all concerned, providing they weighed less than six tons!

Naturally, there are always those who consider themselves to be exceptions to any rule and sadly Mr. William Burley was about to attempt to qualify as a special case. William was the patriarch of the Burley family, the owners of the local bus company who operated an excellent service between Selby and York with their 'majestic' coaches. He had taken the trouble to acquaint father with the fact that a new bus about to be delivered 'was a bit heavier than usual' but appeared a little uncertain as to its actual weight. 'If it's over six tons it's not coming over this bridge', said father with great conviction, and the most burly of the Burley's retreated in disorder without uttering another word.

The new bus was duly delivered to gasps of admiration from the local fare-paying public which at the time meant almost everyone in the village, including father on his regular Saturday trips to the Upper Circle at York's Empire Theatre. For several weeks and for some quite inexplicable reason, the new bus plied between Selby and Cawood, the bemused passengers disembarking at the firm's garage in the village, there to join another bus in order to continue their journey via the bridge to York.

Quite naturally the Bridgemaster was aware of Mr. Burley's reluctance to venture across Cawood Bridge with his new bus but refused to comment on this state of affairs, despite leading questions that came his way from certain local residents. For some reason many of them were now taking an increasing interest in the splendid views of the river from the bridge, using the opportunity of the visit in an attempt to 'draw' the Bridgemaster about Bill Burley's new bus. They failed.

And so it was that one fine sunny evening the Bridgemaster was leaning over the parapet at the Cawood end of the bridge when suddenly there appeared on the

15

East-Riding side the new 'Majestic' bus. Father straightened, a look of astonishment on his face. 'How the hell did he get across? I've been on the bridge since two o'clock', he asked himself aloud.

The bus advanced towards us, travelling slowly, almost reverently, as father quickly buttoned the jacket of his uniform and raised his hand with the signal that says 'Stop!' in any language. The bus drew to a halt and he approached the driver's side. 'Ow do Sid' came a pleasant enough greeting which he chose not to hear. 'What weight are you?' demanded father. 'I don't know Sid but it's written on't side' came the guarded reply.

The trial of strength had arrived and the intrigued passengers watched in silence as the Bridgemaster approached the vehicle's nearside to read the weight — 5 tons 19 cwts! He returned to the driver and pronounced his verdict. 'I'm sorry but this bus can't come over the bridge with more than six passengers aboard' he announced. 'Right Sid, I'll tell the old man' said the driver, with something of an air of menace in his voice, almost as if father had just signed his own death-warrant.

Later that evening a certain schoolboy was finishing homework in the 'front room' at Bridge House when an elderly gentleman was observed tacking somewhat breathlessly along the Castle Wall in the general direction of Bridge House.

There was an angry knock at the door. Fortunately mother had gone to the Women's Institute, while father, who had just raided the larder, was quietly enjoying a plate of bread, cheese and pickles . . . a fuming Mr. Burley was ushered into the living room.

All agog, I listened while the proprietor of the 'Majestic' Bus Service explained the difficulty of constructing a modern bus with a weight that fell beneath the unfeeling limits laid down by the West Riding County Council. Father sympathised but explained that his duty was clear, and what's more, he had no choice in the matter. If the bus and its occupants were over six tons in weight, it could not pass over Cawood Bridge. 'But the lad tells me that all but six passengers have got to walk over the bridge' continued a harassed Mr. Burley. 'Better that than they find themselves floating down the river' came father's uncompromising reply. 'Anyway you knew the position before you ordered the damn bus'.

The conversation was becoming heated and I eased open the door slightly in anticipation of the fireworks that I felt certain were to follow. 'I'll see you to the door' said father indicating that he considered the interview was at an end. Mr. Burley got to his feet and puffed over to the door, producing a five-pound note as he went. 'I'm sure we can sort this out Sid', he said as he attempted to push the now folded fiver into the top pocket of father's uniform jacket. 'Get out!' yelled father and a startled Mr. Burley made a hasty and most undignified exit, still clutching the precious five-pound note.

So ended the saga of the new 'Majestic' bus and why, ever since, all but six fortunate passengers have walked across Cawood Bridge.

*   *   *   *   *

'What the devil's that?' said father rising from the breakfast table in surprise as Bridge House began to suddenly reverberate with the noise of powerful engines. He opened the door and gasped in astonishment! The street was full of tanks the leading one now at the foot of the bridge with its hatch open, a fresh-faced young officer reading the incriminating bridge sign — 'Weight Limit 6 Tons!'

Hastily donning his uniform jacket and peaked cap he left the house, striding purposefully towards the leading tank. 'We are coming over' shouted the young lieutenant eagerly above the roar of the engines whose exhausts were rapidly turning the High Street into a blue haze. 'Oh no you are not. There's a weight limit of six tons on this bridge!' bawled the Bridgemaster in reply. 'Don't you realise there is a bloody war on' countered the young officer angrily as he attempted to vacate the tank's turret, promptly tripped, and fell sprawling into the roadway.

He scrambled to his feet and glared at the small group of curious villagers who had now gathered to watch the proceedings. Somewhat bemused, father beckoned him to one side in the direction of the bridge. 'What weight are you?' he demanded, as the unfortunate officer rubbed his bruised elbow. 'Twenty-two tons' volunteered our gallant tank commander, a little lamely, 'but we are still going over the bridge'. 'Oh no you're not' replied father 'at least not until I have authority from County Hall, and whilst you think about it, you might tell your men to switch off their engines. You're wasting petrol and gassing the street!'

The lieutenant turned angrily on his heel and returned towards the safety of his tank just as a second head appeared in the turret. The officer beckoned him down. There was a short conversation and the corporal trotted smartly off down the line of tanks and engines were turned off as an uneasy silence descended on the street. The young officer returned to the fray. 'You are holding up the war; you could be shot for this!' he remonstrated. Father eyed him coldly. 'You attempt to take one of those tanks over this bridge and you are the one who's likely to get shot' he replied evenly.

'Is there a Police Station in the village' asked the officer, addressing one of the bystanders, who promptly turned his back and walked away. The lieutenant tried again. 'Bridgemaster, do you think I might use your telephone?', he enquired almost politely. 'You could if we had one' said father. 'Are you trying to tell me this bridge is not on the telephone?' he demanded incredulously. 'I am not "trying" to tell you. I am telling you' retorted father turning on his heel, and marching onto the bridge. He reached the gate that closed the bridge to road traffic when it was about to be opened and slammed the gate shut with a final gesture of defiance.

The procession of tanks was now causing a considerable stir in the village, the column stretching back past the Market Place and into Sherburn Street, their crews anxious to exercise cramped limbs and gratefully accepting the numerous cups of precious tea that were being handed round by the villagers with their typical Yorkshire hospitality.

Meanwhile, back at the bridge something more than half an hour had elapsed since the departure of the lieutenant on his way to 'fetch the police'. This was not to be wondered at since he had been misdirected at the

'You are holding up the war; you could be shot for this!'

Corner End where he should have turned left for the Police Station instead of right. He ended up at the Cemetery Lodge on the outskirts of the village. Here, Harry Frankish had great difficulty in convincing him that his bungalow was not the Police Station, but, as Harry said later, 'I told him he were welcome 'cos I still 'ave plenty of room!'

19

The Bridgemaster left his vantage point on the gate of the bridge as P.C. Wilkes was spotted together with his now limping military escort as they headed along the Castle Wall in the direction of the bridge. The latter gentleman appeared somewhat heated and was indulging in much arm-waving, leaving P.C. Wilkes to concentrate on the job in hand — that of pushing his pedal cycle!

'Now Sid', said P.C. Wilkes as the parties arrived in 'no-man's land' at the foot of the bridge, 'we seem to have a bit of a problem'. 'There's no problem as far as I am concerned' retorted father. 'They can go round by Tadcaster or Selby but they are not bringing twenty-ton tanks over this bridge with its six-ton limit'. P.C. Wilkes looked appealingly at the source of the trouble. 'It does seem to me sir, you have a great deal at stake. If one of them tanks finishes up in the river it could be awkward, not only for you and the likely damage to the bridge, but also for the chaps inside the thing as well!'

'I am perfectly certain that the bridge is strong enough to take our weight' insisted the limping lieutenant who was now wishing he'd never heard of a county called Yorkshire, let alone been ordered to serve in it! 'Oh I see' said father, unable to resist rubbing a little salt into the wound. 'We are an engineer now are we, as well as a tank driver!'

'Look Sid' said P.C. Wilkes in desperation, 'this is getting us nowhere!' Father was also becoming impatient; he should have re-baited his eel-lines hours ago. The lines would be in a devil of a mess with the overnight catch still on them. It was time for action and for surnames. 'Wilkes!' he said, 'I've told him once and I tell you now. The only way those tanks go over this bridge is with County Hall permission, so the sooner you get back to the station and ring Wakefield, the better for all of us. I told young 'Lord Kitchener' that over an hour ago and that's my final word.' With that, he turned smartly on his heel and marched back onto the bridge.

The young officer looked appealingly in the direction of P.C. Wilkes. Clearly, his enforced march around the village, coupled with his fall from the tank, had exhausted him. 'I'm sure I can leave the job of telephoning in your capable hands officer', he said hopefully. 'No!,

I'm afraid you can't sir' replied the worthy constable. 'I shall need to act as a witness to the conversation. After all — they are your tanks'.

The Bridgemaster watched in silence as the deputation started slowly back along the Castle Wall en route for the police station. Then, walking quickly back to the cabin, he collected his bait bucket and sack and set off for his eel-lines on the nearby riverbank. He returned some ten minutes later with a sackful of thrashing eels. 'Go and get my two-foot rule and a newspaper,' he ordered, 'I've just caught the biggest eel of my life.' The eel was laid out on the newspaper, a favourite trick of father's to stop them wriggling. 'Forty-seven inches' he announced triumphantly as he folded up his joiner's rule. 'That must be the biggest fresh-water eel that's ever been caught round here — let's go and have a cup of tea and tell mother'.

It was nearly two hours before Mr. Wilkes returned on his cycle, this time without his military escort. 'It's alright Sid, but they have got to go over the bridge dead slow and one at a time.' he said. 'What's happened to young "Lord Kitchener?"' asked father beaming! This rather surprised P.C. Wilkes in the circumstances . . . but then he didn't know about the eel! 'Oh, he's coming in his own time. He seems a bit lame' replied a relieved P.C. Wilkes.

The crews climbed aboard their tanks, engines were started and the villagers waved their 'goodbyes', as one by one the tanks crawled slowly over the bridge and continued on their way to war. As the last one disappeared over into the East Riding in a cloud of smoke and dust, one local sage was heard to remark, 'Never in the field of human conflict, were so many held up for so long, by so few!'

Welcome to Wales

It was the spring of 1941 and the war was going badly, or so said father as he tossed 'The People' newspaper angrily aside in obvious disgust. Previous successes in the Middle East against the Italians had been countered by the Germans who were now advancing on Tobruk. They had also managed to invade Greece and Yugoslavia. At sea the country was facing terrible losses to merchant shipping due to mines and 'U' boats whilst at home the German 'blitz' brought nightly terror to London and other major cities causing terrible destruction and great loss of life.

'If it goes on much longer like this we shall be bunkastered' said father angrily. Mother nodded in agreement and continued with her pea-shelling operations for the Sunday dinner. I didn't know what 'bunkastered' meant but from the look on father's face it was obvious it was something pretty serious. 'We have got two new four-engined bombers the Stirling and the Halifax now Dad', I added hopefully. He grunted and left the house, doubtless to review the deteriorating War situation with his cronies on the bridge.

He was to remain in sombre mood for several weeks until the Sunday morning that mother announced 'We are all going to Wales in August for a holiday!' Father dropped the Sunday paper in astonishment. 'Whatever are you thinking about lass. We can't go off on holiday in the middle of a war!' he demanded angrily. 'And why not?' retorted mother. I don't see why that man Hitler should prevent me and the children from seeing mother and the family and you don't have to come if you don't want to'. Father looked glum, and for once it seemed as if he had lost his usual role as decision maker for the family.

I found him some minutes later leaning dejectedly over the parapet of the bridge apparently deep in thought. He eyed me as I joined him. 'Thee mam's made up her mind lad, so's there's nowt we can do' he said sadly, as if going to Wales was some sort of punishment. 'Well that's that then dad', I added sympathetically, my heart beating with excitement. The decision gave new meaning to my role as village butcher boy! Mr. Kettlewood the butcher had doubled my wages when he took over the shop and choirboy fees at church had recently been increased to sixpence a Service. With any luck I would be a near-millionaire by the time August arrived!

Now there was something else to think about apart from the war, for mother was a great strategist as well as a planner. Trunks and cases had to be roped or strapped with father playing the leading role as luggage was got ready to be 'sent in advance' with him marching dutifully to the local railway station to 'fix things up' with Harry Oldfield the station-master.

The great day arrived at last and the family trooped over the bridge in the early morning sunshine to the nearby home of Mr. Hargraves who had been charged with the task of driving us to York in time for the 7 o'clock train. We climbed hastily aboard his smart little red and black Morris 8 Saloon and chugged off down the Ferry Lane, the speedometer of the car rotating like a ship's compass on a gimbal; clearly Mr. Morris felt his latest creation deserved something better than a mere pointer to register the speed! On arrival at York mother handed Mr. Hargraves a precious ten-shilling note in appreciation of services rendered and we exchanged thanks and said our good-byes.

There was a friendly smile and a nod from two giant 'redcaps' as we entered the station that was crowded with travellers, even at this early hour. Father eyed the groups of service personnel with their rifles and kit-bags with a certain unease. 'It don't seem right Ruth that we are going on holiday with all these lads going off to war', father remonstrated. 'If you only knew' demanded mother, 'most of them are going on leave like we are', and father lapsed into a sullen silence.

I was quick to notice that much of the glass in the station roof was missing, the roof being covered by an assortment of ancient tarpaulins. For some reason the Germans didn't appear to like York Station! They even managed to bomb it in daylight one murky Sunday afternoon when a parachute mine conveniently landed on soft ground in the gardens nearby causing far less damage than might have been expected.

The station fascinated me. It was a far cry from Cawood's single track Goods line that only brought passenger coaches once a year for the Sunday School outing to Bridlington; a day that Mr. Oldfield the station master always dreaded. He had to spend much of the Friday evening chasing off the hordes of excited children who were determined to swarm all over them!

York Station was quite different. Here were giant engines the like of which I had never seen before, many thundering through the station without reducing speed, a shrill whistle telling York that they were too busy to stop and call today. Then, a huge engine appeared at our platform clanking and wheezing with the effort of pulling a string of green carriages that all seemed to be joined together with what looked like a giant bellows between each. There were large painted numbers on the doors that decreed whether you travelled 1st, 2nd or 3rd class. The 3rd class Booths climbed hastily aboard, doors slammed, whistles blew, and the Guard on the platform waved a green flag as he replaced a large watch in his waistcoat pocket and stepped neatly aboard the now moving train. 'She's dead on time' said father leaning on the open window of the carriage door as we slowly passed a giant clock suspended from the station roof. 'Oh yes!' continued father 'The London North Eastern has a schedule to keep and if Hitler and any of his misguided countrymen have any thoughts about interfering with that, then they had better think again!' He returned comforted to his seat in the carriage and I remained in the swaying corridor as the fields and farms of Yorkshire flashed past the window as we hurried south towards Sheffield.

The day War broke out

We found the city little worse for its encounter with the enemy, or at least as far as we could tell from the railway. The factory chimneys were smoking busily and the wheels above the distant coal mines were spinning merrily as Yorkshire got on with the job of winning the war. 'Wait 'till I see that fool who told me Sheffield were flattened' said father heatedly as he returned once more to his seat in the carriage as I continued to watch with youthful fascination as the factories and workshops sped by in the landscape below.

We soon exchanged the green livery of the London and North Eastern for the maroon of the London Midland and Scottish as we thundered through the 'Black Country' and the industrial heart of Britain until we reached Shropshire's broad acres and the county town of Shrewsbury. Here the chocolate and cream of the Great Western Railway was very much in evidence.

At Craven Arms, the first of mother's brothers met the train and there was a joyful re-union; for Fred, Will and Jeff all worked for the Great Western explained mother proudly. Leominster was reached in the late afternoon-or 'Lemster' should you be unfamiliar with the correct pronunciation as most of us appeared to be. Waiting on the platform as we left the train was Uncle Jeff in his shiny topped driver's hat. Then it was across the park for tea with aunt and the family with an hour to wait before we could continue with the final stage of our journey.

'I think Will may be driving you up to New Radnor' said Uncle Jeff with a mouthful of muffin. Here was the evidence that the Great Western Railway in this part of the world was very much a family affair. And so it proved to be later with Uncle Will kissing everyone in sight several times over. Mother's side of the family certainly appeared to be very affectionate. I mentioned to father later that this was the first time I had seen grown men kissing each other, even if they were brothers or brothers-in-law! I waited for father's response but for once he seemed a little at a loss for words — he was still getting over the shock!

The journey from Leominster to New Radnor seemed to take an age, the train stopping every few miles at tiny wayside stations and halts, their neat allotment gardens

26

Welcome to Wales

ranged along the line. Passengers came and went, for no one ran a car in Britain now unless the essential nature of their work demanded it, so car ownership was still some thing of a pipe dream for most ordinary working folk.

We reached Kington with time for Uncle Will to wander along the platform to our carriage for a chat. He was smaller than Uncle Jeff with a ruddy complexion and a generous but neat moustache. For some reason he preferred a flat cap, rather than the peaked one I associated with the important people who drove railway engines. He stood talking quietly to his long absent sister, wiping his hands on a piece of cotton-waste and puffing gently on his pipe.

'Would you like to ride on the engine boy? he asked, a twinkle in his eye. I was already half-way down the platform when he called me back. 'No, not here boy, when we reach Stanner Halt!' he said hastily. As I climbed excitedly aboard the engine at Stanner he explained that I must get down at Dolyhir the next stop for it was against Company rules for mere mortals to ride on the foot-plate. New Radnor was next explained Uncle, and it wouldn't do for the new station master to see me riding on the engine.

We reached New Radnor just after six o'clock on a sunny August evening and father handed the ticket to a station master who looked like an Admiral of the Fleet with lots of gold braid on his hat and sleeves. His porter was busy unloading countless squeaking boxes marked 'Day old Chicks — Handle with Care'. Behind them in the Guard's van were several large wicker baskets of pigeons who gazed reproachfully at us as they quietly waited their turn to be unloaded.

As I gazed around in wonder at the mountains I had the distinct impression that somehow the Good Lord had taken special care with this part of his creation. Father also appeared to sense the emotion of the moment and turning to mother he said quietly, 'Welcome back to Wales lass!' Mother sniffed and brushed away a tear, the war forgotten, for in a few minutes we would reach Grandma's little cottage in the 'Dingle' and all would be well with the world.

As we walked on into the village and over the bridge (which locals say will always bring you back if you walk over it) I remembered the brook from a visit some years earlier. Even today, it still gurgles happily down the side of the village street, clear as crystal and cold as ice, with fat little trout lying under stones.

When Grandma announced at breakfast on Sunday morning that all present would be expected to attend Morning Service I was neither surprised, nor dismayed. Sometime later we all set off down the 'Dingle' wearing our 'Sunday-best' with my young cousin carrying a music-case.

As we entered the church she hastily left the party in response to a command of 'off you go my girl' from Grandma and marched resolutely over to the organ. Seating herself on the bench she began to play with what I considered was remarkable ability as people began to enter the church in readiness for the Service.

'. . . her twin pig-tails dancing merrily as she strained for the base pedals beneath her feet.'

'Well I'll be da . . . blessed!' exclaimed father in astonishment, as he collected a sharp dig in the ribs and a reproachful glance from mother.

'Give it some stick lad', whispered father as the first hymn started with young Irene working energetically away at the organ, her twin pig-tails dancing merrily as she strained for the base pedals beneath her feet. And sing we did, with a bemused Sir Henry and Lady Duff-Gordon in the front pew turning heads slightly to see where the new choral support was coming from!

That afternoon there was great excitement with the arrival of Uncle Hedley and Aunty May with their pony and trap and the news that we were to return with them to Honeysuckle Farm. Uncle Hedley's farm was the nearest thing to paradise that a boy could wish for. There were cows and sheep, pigs and chickens, lots of rabbits, and a brook full of big fat trout that I could never seem to catch with my rod, but which Uncle seemed quite happy to catch with his hands!

Uncle was very attached to his pony and showed me how to feed him an apple with palm extended and fingers closed together. 'You can ride him bareback when we get home boy' said Uncle enthusiastically. 'He's a very intelligent pony and I've even taught him to read!' I eyed him dubiously, for I had a great affection for Uncle Hedley and he wasn't the sort of person to tell fibs. He looked hurt. 'Just you wait until we go back tonight boy, then you will see whether he can read or not'.

After a tea of raspberries and cream we three youngsters climbed aboard the trap and the party set off for the return trip to Honeysuckle Farm, with Uncle driving. He insisted that I sat opposite him at the front so that I might witness his pony's ability to read road-signs.

At the bottom of the 'Dingle' there was a 'Halt' sign at the junction with the main road and this said Uncle was where he would demonstrate his clever pony's ability to read. As we approached, Uncle ordered everyone to be silent and dropped the reins. Sure enough, as we reached the junction, the pony suddenly stopped dead, turned his head slightly back towards the trap as if to say 'How about that!' and Uncle took up the reins again and we trotted off down the road.

'*He's a very intelligent pony and I've even taught him to read!*'

The journey back to the farm took the best part of an hour, for we had to climb the steep bank into Old Radnor and then on and down into Burlingjobb, the farm lying below us in the valley as we descended the mountain.

On arrival, we were sent to fetch the cows as Uncle busied himself with releasing the pony and hanging up the harness. He milked about four cows in his tiny cowshed, sitting on a little three-legged stool with the bucket gripped firmly between his knees. Sometimes, he would squirt us with a stream of hot milk that never failed to hit me in the eye as we stood watching fascinated in the doorway. We helped by carrying the buckets of steaming milk across the yard and along the garden path to the dairy attached to the house, later to be 'separated' by aunt, who it seemed, enjoyed an enviable local reputation as a butter-maker.

The girls 'turned the cows out' and disappeared in the direction of the brook. I had discovered a small hutch in the corner of the yard that contained two tiny furry creatures that I imagined were ferrets, although I had never seen a live ferret before. 'Don't put your finger through the wire; they bite!' shouted Uncle from the direction of the cowshed, as he hastened across the yard. He raised the flap on the top of the cage and removed one of the ferrets by the scruff of the neck and proceeded to rub its back gently with his fingers. The ferret was pale yellow in colour and I noticed he had two rows of tiny needle-sharp teeth.

'Would you like to go rabbiting?' asked Uncle eagerly, as he dropped master ferret back into the cage and it was clear from his manner that he would require little encouragement from me. We set off with me carrying a large shoulder bag containing the nets while Uncle marched ahead with master ferret peering out from a large side pocket in his coat as he sniffed the air expectantly.

We arrived at the warren, a large bank covered with numerous rabbit holes and fresh droppings that indicated the residents were at home. 'Empty out the nets' commanded Uncle dropping young 'Ferdinand' into the bag and pulling the draw strings tight to prevent his escape. For several minutes Uncle busied himself, placing nets

31

over the surrounding rabbit holes, fixing them to the ground with the pegs and cord attached to the nets.

'Come on boy' said Uncle encouragingly, opening the sack and seizing Ferdinand by the scruff of the neck. He popped him into one of the open holes near the top of the bank and Ferdinand promptly turned round and came out again! He received a sharp 'talking to' from his master and was once again thrust into the hole. We lay quietly on the bank for several minutes with Uncle listening intently. Again Ferdinand appeared at a nearby hole, somewhat concerned about the net that now appeared to be impeding his exit. 'Drat!' said Uncle seizing the unfortunate ferret and pushing him down a netted hole much lower on the bank. Clearly, his efforts to initiate his young nephew into the mysteries of rabbit-catching were not going according to plan.

Uncle was again listening intently with his ear to the ground. Then he smiled and whispered. 'He's found 'em boy. You can hear 'em thumping. They are warning each other of danger!' With ear to the ground I too could hear the urgent thumping from below.

Suddenly there was an eruption from the surrounding holes with rabbits running away in all directions apart from the half dozen or so that had chosen the wrong exits and were now struggling frantically in the nets to free themselves. Uncle dealt quickly and methodically with each net in turn — all except the last one. Here the fortunate rabbit managed to free himself from the net and quickly made his escape down the meadow . . . and I felt glad!

It was quite some time before Ferdinand re-appeared, blinking in the last rays of the evening sunshine and seemingly quite unaware of the chaos he had just created in this part of the animal kingdom. Back he went into the familiar pocket and we set off down the meadow towards the nearby farm with Ferdinand still continuing to admire the view and me carrying the precious rabbits.

I was up very early the next morning to a breakfast of home-cured bacon and eggs cooked on an ancient twin burner 'Valour' paraffin stove that smoked like a garden bonfire! Aunt was soon busy in the dairy and I received orders to visit the garden to collect a basket full of loganberries for a pie, although I had never seen these strange fruits before that resemble large raspberries and are somewhat bitter.

As I worked happily away at my fruit-picking chore, I heard what appeared to be voices coming from the 'privy' at the top of the garden. I had visited this noble edifice the previous evening and noticed the side-by-side 'seating' with its choice of sizes, but not in my wildest dreams had I imagined that both were likely to be occupied at the same time! The only other possibility was that Uncle was talking to himself, albeit somewhat loudly.

Keeping to the garden in case the door of the 'privy' should suddenly be opened, I advanced quickly to within earshot and recognised the second voice. It was Mr. Bradley who lived next door. What was he doing in Uncle Hedley's privy? What was more sinister — what was Uncle Hedley doing in there with him. . .?

Suddenly, the door opened and Uncle appeared with a copy of the morning paper under his arm and marched off down the path in the direction of the farmhouse. Still feeling somewhat nonplussed I returned to my fruit picking in time to see Mr. Bradley emerge from his 'station' on the other side of the fence also with a paper tucked under his arm.

It transpired that both men kept this vital morning 'appointment' at about the same time each day. They sat 'back-to-back' so to speak, in their respective 'privies' having knocked out a couple of bricks high on the wall above their heads, thus enabling them to read and happily converse together as they sat comfortably discussing the latest war news in their daily papers.

I spent much time at the brook in the days that followed, but try as I might I failed to catch any of its elusive brown trout. Matters were made worse by Uncle who would join me on the bank on his way home from the Gore quarry. Lying face down near a conveniently overhanging tree, he would quickly scoop out several large trout with his hands with the comment 'Don't say I caught 'em boy', certain in the belief that all fishermen were storytellers.

Honeysuckle Farm had one other permanent resident apart from Aunt and Uncle. This was old Mr. Payne who

33

worked at the 'Strings' quarry down the road and often helped about the farm. 'He is a fine fisherman' commented Uncle as he watched me dejectedly fishing one evening. 'Would you like me to ask him if he will take you fishing tomorrow night?.

The next evening I waited impatiently for Mr. Payne to finish his tea and even more impatiently as he produced a long but battered greenheart rod and proceeded to 'tackle up'. He seemed a very old man with a droopy moustache and always wore the same ancient grease-stained trilby hat. Clearly, not a man for half-measures, Mr. Payne wore a belt as well as braces and also supported his corduroy trousers with two pieces of binder twine tied round his legs just below the knee.

We set off for the brook with something dangling from the end of his line that looked like a miniature torpedo with a small propeller blade attached either side and a mass of hooks that seemed big enough to catch a whale! Uncle Hedley was a great one for practical jokes. Surely he wasn't fooling me with Mr. Payne!

We reached the brook and Mr Payne positioned me on a foot-bridge and clambered over the handrail to stand on a little island of shingle in the middle. Crooking his arm around his giant rod, he proceeded to fill and light a battered old briar pipe. He puffed away until the pipe was drawing satisfactorily and dropped his tangle of hooks into the stream with a gentle 'plop'.

Where he was fishing, the water could not have been more than a foot in depth but he proceeded to wave the rod from side to side, the 'bait' travelling back and forth like a silvery dart in the water. I watched his actions more in surprise than fascination, for I could not believe that this strange display would result in him catching anything! I must tell Uncle about Mr. Payne's ineptitude with a rod; the poor old chap really has no idea!

My concentration wandered for a moment, my eyes following the movement of sheep on the mountain opposite. Then it happened. There was a sudden flurry of water, the end of the rod tipped skywards and out of the brook came the largest trout I had ever seen! Mr. Payne did not appear in the least surprised. Quickly removing the hook, he killed the fish instantly, and threw it

'*Mr Payne wasn't a fisherman — he was a magician!*'

towards my direction on the bank with the words 'Well, there's the cock, now let's see if we can catch his mate'. He quietly returned to his rod-waving and within a matter of minutes, a second and even larger trout joined its companion on the bank at my feet. I regarded Mr. Payne with awe. He wasn't a fisherman . . . he was a magician!

We walked back with me carrying the fish threaded cleverly onto a hazel twig. When we reached the farm, Mr. Payne inspected my fishing tackle with much head shaking. He explained that float tackle was no use on fast flowing mountain streams where there was so much variation in the speed and the depth of the water. What was needed was just a single weight that would carry the bait down. Throw the line upstream and allow it to swim down into the pool explained Mr. Payne. The bait was not really suitable either. Worms were fine when there was some colour in the water he explained but in fine clear weather wasp grubs were much better.

The following evening Uncle Hedley found a wasp's nest, popped something down the hole that looked like a round glacier mint, poured water down after it and beat a hasty retreat. About an hour later we returned to the nest and uncle dug it up. The pieces of wasp comb were placed on an old tin plate in the oven and roasted for some minutes, otherwise said uncle, the wasps would remain alive and you will find yourself baiting with live wasps!

We returned to the brook as the sun was setting, the ideal time, explained Mr. Payne. He watched me catch my first trout, nodded approvingly and then disappeared in the direction of the farm. As darkness descended, I trudged happily homeward through the water meadows with six fine trout dangling from a hazel twig. Mr. Payne spent the next evening with me and taught me more about the habits of the brown trout. How each has his own 'lying' position on warm days with the choicest spot being claimed by the largest fish. 'Catch the big 'un, and in a few days his place in the sun will be taken over by the next largest fish' he said. He read the brook like a book, his knowledge of the fish and their habits as extensive as it was remarkable.

Mr. Payne is long since dead, but I still fish his brook, often sitting quietly by the stream as the shadows lengthen with the silence broken only by the occasional call of a sheep or the distant bark of a dog. Catching trout now seems quite unimportant, for here there is an inner peace and tranquility that for me relates to better men and better times, far removed from the bustle and grab of today's world. People do matter more than things. . . . I for one, shall never forget old Harry Payne.

*　　　　*　　　　*　　　　*　　　　*

We were enjoying a hot spell of summer weather.
'Hedley, whenever are you going to see to those bees?' demanded Aunty May who, it would seem, was the great regulator in the Evan's household. 'Alright, alright May', said Uncle heatedly, 'I'll do them tonight, although there's thunder about.' Father was busy splitting firewood and even Uncle Hedley had a look of admiration in his eyes for the professional way in which father located the various metal wedges. He had gone early to the quarry that Saturday morning and was therefore unaware of father's concern about the condition of 'poor Hedley's tools'.

'These wedges wouldn't cut butter' had been father's comment as he examined the contents of the tool-shed, and the first part of the morning had been spent with me turning the handle of the grindstone while father sharpened everything in sight! He brought a wealth of experience to the task. At home, most of our winter fuel came floating up the river in the shape of dead trees which he lassoed from the bridge. We cut them up on the 'cobbles' with his giant cross-cut saw as the tide went out, the wedge-work and splitting coming later.

The bees lived in 'the nursery' a small field bounded by sheer cliffs on one side and providing a sheltered location for young stock as well as a home for Aunty May's hens. Father expressed great interest in the expedition to 'take the bees' and the three of us set off with me carrying the empty 'super'. Uncle Hedley was kept busy attempting to ignite the 'puffer' as we walked up through the meadow. This was a sort of bellows with a metal spout filled with

37

a rolled up newspaper, which when lit and working properly gives off volumes of white smoke like the chimney of a railway engine.

'You don't wear a veil then Hedley' commented father warily, an indication that he had some knowledge of the task ahead. 'No! No! Sid, I don't find it necessary' said Uncle, angrily fiddling with his puffer which kept managing to go out, just as it seemed he had built up a reasonable head of steam. We arrived at the hives and on uncle's advice, positioned ourselves on a little hillock some fifteen or twenty yards from the danger zone and sat down to watch. Uncle 'puffed' away at a hive for several minutes, his actions producing a 'damn' or a 'drat you' as an offending bee was swept off his arm. He removed the top of the hive and just as he began to puff the interior, he ran out of smoke and had to retire to relight his puffer. The delay hardly worked to his advantage!

On his return to the hive the now angry bees were waiting for him but he gamely continued, despite the fact that there now seemed to be more bees about his person than anywhere else. Matters became even worse when he attempted to remove the honey laden panels. It had been a good season and it seemed that the industrious bees had managed to weld some of them together.

He now became impatient, fighting to remove the sticking panels, the hive rocking dangerously, the angry bees losing no opportunity to register their protests on the most unlikely parts of his anatomy.

Father found the proceedings highly entertaining and was roaring with laughter until a detachment of angry bees decided to concentrate their efforts on the perimeter of the hives and for some reason decided that he must be responsible for the carnage below. Father's departure from the scene was a sight I shall never forget. One moment he was helpless with mirth — the next he was racing off down the meadow with the speed of an Olympic runner, a swarm of angry bees in hot pursuit!

'Never mind boy, we took 'em' said Uncle Hedley later as he sat with me on the old school seat in the front garden of the farm and I churned happily away on the handle of the extractor, the honey spattering against the sides of the drum. His face was already puffed and swollen, giving him the appearance of something out of a 'horror' movie. I said how sorry I was that he had been stung so badly. 'These are easier to bear than your Aunt's tongue', he said philosophically, 'and anyway, bee stings is good for you'.

The following Saturday we left Wales at the start of our long journey back to Yorkshire. For two whole weeks the war had seemed far away, almost forgotten, but now it was time to return. 'War or no war', said father quietly, 'it will be good to get home again'.

The Wager

In the tiny Snug bar of the Ferry House Inn on some evenings in the week and often on Sundays would be found local farmer, District Scout Commissioner and head of the Selby Special Constabulary, Roger Noel Richardson. Roger owned a charming house and compact farm within stone-throwing distance of the Parish Church and was at this time embarking upon a new venture as a commercial mushroom grower.

He was well known in the district and held in high regard by my generation in the village who saw in him the personification of success. He owned a Riley Sports Saloon and was one of the first of our local farmers to employ one of the new Allis Chalmers tractors when most of his contemporaries were still at the horse and cart stage.

On this particular Sunday evening Roger was at the Ferry House and as I had to see him about a Scouting matter I was allowed through the bar to the Snug. I found him in deep conversation with Paddy, a tall, good looking Irishman, wearing a dark blue uniform and Pilot's wings of the Air Transport Auxiliary.

It seemed that our mounting bomber offensive against Germany was the topic of conversation and Paddy was extolling the virtues of the new Lancaster bomber. Roger, ever controversial, was stoutly defending the record and performance of the Halifax, which, he said, was a much better aircraft.

Paddy remarked that he was collecting a Lancaster the following day for delivery to a squadron and would be flying into Sherburn around 5 o'clock in the afternoon. The Ferry pilots had their base at Sherburn-in-Elmet, a small village some five miles from Cawood and adjoining Blackburn's new aircraft factory, which was busily engaged in the construction and repair of Swordfish and Albacore Aircraft for the Fleet. Roger suggested that as Paddy would be in the vicinity with his wonderful Lancaster the following day, he may as well demonstrate its versatility by flying it low over the farm. Paddy remarked that he would be just as happy to fly the ruddy thing under the telephone wires near the bridge!

This brought an immediate response from Roger; 'I'll bet you a fiver you can't.' And so the wager was laid with Landlord Walter Green being asked to hold the two large white old fashioned five pound notes, representing at that time the best part of a month's wages for most of the working men in the village. I remained unnoticed in the doorway to the Snug as the conversation progressed and decided to sneak away with my secret information that promised the thrill of a lifetime the following day, for, in common with most of my generation, I was aeroplane mad, or so said my father.

Crossing the river just below the bridge at Cawood there used to be two huge steel pylons that locals said carried the main telephone lines between Leeds and York. I remember that at school we once measured their height as a 'geometrical' exercise and they each proved to be exactly one hundred and thirty-five feet. It seems their quite excessive height had been decided upon at the turn of the century to ensure that the masts of passing sailing barges would not damage them, although I could never remember seeing a barge with a mast much over fifty feet in height.

The masts were a great attraction to the youth of the village for it was possible to climb them on the inside as far as the cross-braces about two thirds of the way up, which somehow did not seem quite so dangerous as climbing up the outside! They were positioned either side of the river some four hundred yards down-stream from the bridge. Bridge House where we lived adjoined the bridge and had been constructed so that the large living room window provided an uninterrupted view of the river almost as far as Wharfe Mouth, where this Dale's tributary enters the River Ouse.

'And so the wager was laid!'

I spent much of Sunday evening, wondering whether I ought to feign illness the following day, for school was at Selby some five miles away and the afternoon bus might well be late, by which time the intended event could have taken place. I made a half-hearted attempt at feeling unwell on Monday morning, declining breakfast and complaining of a sore throat. I should have remembered mother's home nursing training. My tongue was duly inspected and pronounced satisfactory and her thermometer confirmed that my temperature was normal. When she said 'We had better see what your father says when he comes in', I knew my cause was lost, and intimated that I was now feeling better and even managed to eat some breakfast!

I arrived home from school at the usual time on Monday afternoon and was fairly certain from father's attitude that the intended event had not yet taken place. During tea, I kept a watchful eye on both river and sky for I was certain that Paddy would make his approach down river from the York side where the river follows a fairly straight course for the best part of half a mile. Tea ended, and father commented that the tide was due. Easing his chair back from the table he replaced his uniform jacket and peaked cap and left the house.

Concealing my excitement, I followed a few moments later, to find him standing on the bridge, his eyes focussed in the direction of the parish church which occupies a commanding position on the bank of the river some eight or nine-hundred yards down-stream. 'A spring tide tonight lad, and a big one', said father. The Ouse at Cawood with a spring tide is a most impressive sight with a wall of water four or five feet high, rushing up the river as fast as a man can run. 'Here she comes', said father, the roar of the water clearly audible before the advancing wave had rounded the bend near the church.

At that precise moment something made me turn and look up the river — and there she was! Paddy and his Lancaster were racing towards us and the incredible thing was, the aircraft was below the level of the banks with the slip stream from her four Merlin engines rippling the waters of the now stilled river. Surprisingly, I could hear no sound from the aircraft but realised that if she did not soon start to lift, Paddy would hit the bridge.

As the tidal wave passed beneath the bridge, father turned to watch its progress onward up the river and as he did so, his eye caught the Lancaster, now less than three hundred yards away and already lifting to clear the bridge. 'Get down!' yelled father, muttering under his breath 'the bloody fool' before smartly prostrating himself on the decking of the bridge. I stood transfixed, watching the most breathtaking piece of flying I had ever seen, as the giant aircraft roared over the bridge just above our heads, passed cleanly under the wires, executed a gentle climbing turn to port, missed the tower of the parish church by what appeared to be inches and disappeared behind a clump of trees. Father picked himself up, more furious than afraid, 'Did you get his bloody number? I'll see to it he never flies again; he damn near

'I stood transfixed, watching the most breathtaking piece of flying I had ever seen . . .'

hit the bridge'. For several minutes father's anger knew no bounds — some idiotic pilot had come within inches of demolishing his precious bridge.

Later that evening P.C. Wilkes presented himself at the Cabin and a record of the incident was duly noted in his dreaded black book, as also was the fact that father had seen Roger waving from the river bank opposite his house. 'I'll do what I can Sid, but without the aircraft's number we can't prove anything', said P.C. Wilkes with a certain lack of enthusiasm, for the local law had every reason to be grateful to father who maintained a some-times lonely nightly vigil in his nice warm cabin on the bridge, but often sharing their company on cold nights.

Knowing of Roger's link with the police in his capacity as I/c of the local Specials, I thought it strange, but per-haps not surprising, that no intelligence of the incident ever filtered through to father. There were celebrations at The Ferry House that night but it was rumoured that 'Mine Host' found it necessary to retire early in some-what bad shape, his place being taken behind the bar by someone wearing a dark blue uniform. As far as I know, nobody ever revealed to father that the incident resulted from a wager made in the Ferry House Inn — right next door to his beloved bridge!

A Chapter of Accidents

The tall, angular figure of Senior Company Officer Robert Moate was standing with his back to the Control Room fire chatting to the ladies of Selby Fire Station when I was ushered into his presence on a cold January morning in 1943. I had just cycled the five miles from my home village to the Station and at sixteen was facing the ordeal of starting my first job.

'This is our new Messenger' announced Chief Moate in a casual and somewhat offhand manner as if he had just found me under a stone and was now determined to make the best of a bad job. 'He will carry messages by cycle to Barlby Fire Station and anywhere else in Selby you care to send him — it should save petrol on the motor cycles', he said. As ladies of the Control Room introduced themselves I was quick to note that Pauline, the junior member of the trio, seemed about my age, although perhaps rather young to be a firewoman.

I was later to realise that the Chief's remarks about petrol savings had quickly reached the ears of Rob and Eddie, the Station's two despatch riders. It transpired that the new Messenger was seen as an immediate threat to Rob and his ancient grey 'Matchless' motor cycle, which usually managed to defy all his efforts to start it in an emergency!

With the introductions over, I was conducted by Senior Company Officer Moate to his private quarters above the Appliance House there to receive my first assignment in the world of work. The room was sparsely furnished and contained two single beds for use by himself and the Station Duty Officer. Near one bed I noticed the large pair of gleaming black fireboots that I had seen him wearing six years previously on my first childhood encounter with a fire engine.

'Now Messenger Booth' ordered my hero of yesteryear, 'I want you to scrub out my quarters every Monday and Thursday and also clean my fireboots. If there has been a fire during the week you will be able to see from their condition that they need cleaning again. See Mrs. Joy in the Control Room and she will fix you up with all the necessary scrubbing gear' he commanded. Pausing for a moment to re-light his pipe, he sniffed loudly (as I later noticed he did when passing on orders of an unpopular or controversial nature) and clattered off down the uncarpeted stairway, leaving behind the most demoralised and dejected employee the National Fire Service had ever recruited.

Leading Firewoman Joy was kind and sympathetic when told of my role as the Station's new 'char-man' and I was provided with a large red fire bucket bearing the word 'Sand' in enormous white letters and containing a scrubbing brush, an ancient chunk of carbolic soap and an evil smelling floor cloth. On reaching the Chief's room brandishing bucket and scrubbing brush I was relieved to find that he had not returned.

For the best part of an hour I attacked the floor with a sullen resentment, spending much time trying to catch the slippery piece of soap as it repeatedly leapt from my unwilling grasp across the water-laden boards. I was saved further misery by the loud ringing of a bell in the Station below. A friendly voice shouted 'Tea Up!' I descended the stairs and was directed to the Mess Room where the duty crew were enjoying their mid-morning break.

On hearing of my 'charring' role, the fireman of Station 6C-3B expressed both astonishment and indignation and various suggestions were put forward. 'Tell him to scrub his own bloody quarters', said Ted, a dour Yorkshireman from Harrogate; 'Shove some bloody newspaper up the toes of his fireboots', said another. 'Why can't one of the women in the Control Room do it?' demanded a third. I felt inclined to agree with all the views expressed by my new found friends who were unanimous that my controversial role was better suited to someone of the opposite sex.

There was young Pauline in the Control Room for instance. She was pretty and pert, yet for some reason her suitability for the task had clearly escaped the notice of Senior Company Officer Moate. 'No bleeding chance mate', confided Eddie, one of the despatch riders. 'Her brother is a Fire Force Commander somewhere or other and anyway she's too young to be in the Service without a bit of pull higher up'. The ring of a bell finally ended the discussion and the group broke up, its members departing to their various tasks about the station.

The following Thursday morning I was attempting a repeat performance on the floor of the Chief's quarters when my aquatic antics came under direct scrutiny. For some reason he decided to visit his room whilst the Thursday 'scrub-out' was in progress and for several seconds he stood in the doorway watching my efforts to recapture the soap, a puzzled expression on his face. Finally, he sniffed loudly, and said 'Messenger Booth, you have no bloody idea how to scrub a floor'. Then, to my astonishment, he shed his uniform jacket, folded it neatly on the nearby bed and sank to his knees on the piece of sacking I was using for a kneeling pad.

For the best part of ten minutes he scrubbed furiously away at the floor, mopping up the dirty water with great sweeps of his arms. With little of the remaining floor left to complete, he suddenly got to his feet with the words 'That's the way to scrub a floor' and, quickly replacing his jacket, sniffed loudly and disappeared down the nearby staircase. I returned to my task with a vigour and enthusiasm that surprised me; Senior Company Officer Moate had brought a new dimension to the work which I was determined to match now there was no pride to get in the way!

My messenger antics at the Station were interesting and sometimes exciting. Frank, the Station Officer, was fairly easy going and his deputy, Reg, a ruddy faced leading fireman was always ready for a friendly chat once official duties were over. It was thanks to Reg that I was able to afford my first motor-cycle, an ancient belt-driven 'Raleigh' complete with three-speed gearbox and bought for the princely sum of ten shillings, or eight hours digging on his allotment; I dug the allotment!

The 'Raleigh' eventually arrived at home in the back of a fire tender that was being used to check fire hydrants in the locality. It was, however, delivered to Nether Farm, courtesy of Roger Richardson, he having readily appreciated that its arrival at Bridge House would not be tolerated by my father. Despite the petrol shortage, the motor cycle enjoyed a new lease of life as it roared up and down the local Inngs, running happily on a mixture of petrol and paraffin. Not surprisingly, word of our clandestine 'goings on' somehow reached the ears of Police Constable Wilkes who made many attempts to catch my friends and myself, but we easily outpaced his pedal cycle and were not in the least averse to taking to the fields for a bit of rough riding when the situation demanded.

Life at the Station in the Park took on a new interest with the arrival of spring and the visits of Column Officer Bailey from Goole with the massive Merryweather Turntable Ladder. On its arrival Senior Company Officer Moate would announce that the duty crew would take part in Turntable Ladder drill. Donning his fireboots, he would rapidly ascend the giant ladder with the agility of a monkey and all eyes would gaze heavenward until he reached the top. Then out would come his beloved pipe, which he calmly proceeded to light whilst standing 'hands-off' on the tiny swaying platform nearly one hundred feet above ground level.

The fire escape proved a great attraction to visitors who sat on nearby seats in the Park, mouths agape as the mighty ladder was put through its paces. On sunny afternoons, the ladies of the Control Room brought out their chairs to observe the proceedings; knitting, chatting, or reading as they watched the non-too-enthusiastic members of the duty crew scramble reluctantly up the giant ladder.

Was there a chance, I mused, that I might be allowed to climb the Escape, a feat bound to be noticed by Pauline, that would perhaps turn a casual interest on her part into something more positive? Certain inner stirrings in recent weeks, not least her smile on my visits to the

Control Room, had led me to the belief that perhaps there were other things in life apart from motor cycles and model aeroplanes!

A plan of campaign was needed if I was to persuade the Chief to let me climb the Escape. He was a person who rarely said 'no', possibly because most of his subordinates found it necessary to keep on the right side of him to avoid confrontation. His agreement to a favourable request was invariably greeted with a 'Yis-Aye'. If I could manage to get 'Ayes' in answer to a couple of fairly straightforward questions, perhaps I could slip in the request about climbing the Merryweather, but I must choose the right moment when he was in a good mood.

A week or so later the ideal opportunity presented itself. An inspection of the station by a visiting dignitary of the now 'nationalised' Fire Service had produced a favourable report and everyone, including the Chief, was in buoyant mood. A special effort was made obvious on the floor of his room that morning; his fireboots shining as they had never shone before. I had even managed to find a piece of carpet for his bedside.

'Morning Messenger Booth' said the Chief breezily. 'Morning Sir' I replied, bringing myself smartly to attention. 'I think we might make a fireman of you yet' he said, casting an approving glance around his quarters. 'Yes Sir, I was wondering whether I might have a word with you about that by asking if you would support my application for student membership of the Institution of Fire Engineers?' 'Certainly' said the Chief, 'anything else?' 'Well Sir, I would like to borrow the new Manuals of Firemanship and also take part in ladder drill the next time Column Officer Bailey brings the Merryweather?' 'Yis aye' he replied — 'See Reg about the Manuals but forget the Escape for a bit — you might break your neck and then your mother would break mine.' He smiled, gave what appeared to be an approving sniff, and disappeared down the stairway leaving me to reconcile myself to the fact that Pauline was to be denied the opportunity of seeing me perform on the turntable-ladder, at least for the time being.

There were other compensating excitements however, not least the morning that Fireman 'Buck' Jones and I were detailed to take the limousine to the Drying Tower to collect hose. The coachbuilt limousine was the old man's pride and joy, delivered to Selby Urban District Council just prior to the outbreak of war and regarded as one of the most up-to-date fire-fighting appliances in service anywhere in the country.

It bristled with gadgetry as well as a heavy duty pump, a first aid hose-reel (with its own mobile water supply) an extending roof ladder and padded red leather seating for the crew that would not have looked out of place in a Rolls Royce. It also towed the station's favourite fire pump, a self-priming Pyrene Pulsometer, except that on this particular morning something was about to go badly wrong with the towing operation.

We left the station with Fireman Jones driving, the trailer pump following obediently behind. Our route to the drying tower lay parallel to the river and as we dipped sharply to pass beneath the local railway bridge, I recoiled with horror from my seat in the back of the vehicle — the trailer pump had vanished! 'Buck, we've lost the pump!' I yelled.

By this time we were climbing the incline on the other side of the dip beneath the bridge, just as the fast moving trailer pump was starting its descent some twenty or so yards behind us. Buck's response to my urgent shout was a rapid application of brakes, the limousine stopped dead, and the wayward pump careered into the back of the vehicle with a grinding crash. Its tow bar suddenly appeared in front of me as the trailer pump burst through the rear doors in a valiant attempt to join me in the back of the towing vehicle.

'Oh my God', cried poor Buck, as he rushed round to the rear of the appliance and gazed in shocked surprise at the twisted remains — 'The old man will bloody kill me!'

By great good fortune, the trailer pump appeared little the worse for its encounter as a high speed battering ram but the same could not be said of the limousine, the force of the impact having torn the lower hinges off both doors that now lay at a drunken angle still attached to the vehicle, each supported by a solitary hinge.

We quickly chocked the rear wheels of the trailer-pump and I wound up the towbar as Buck gently edged

'. . . and the wayward pump careered into the back of the vehicle with a grinding crash . . .'

the limousine forward clear of the pump. After a frantic struggle we managed to close both the shattered rear doors, securing them with a piece of rope. At this I quipped brightly, 'No point in closing the stable door once the pump has gone', a stupid comment that fully deserved the thunderous look I got from Buck as we hitched the pump to the towing vehicle.

We drove back to the station in silence and I could see from the expression on his face that Buck was not looking forward to his coming encounter with the Chief. We pulled up alongside the Appliance House. I sat obediently in the front passenger seat as ordered, while Buck disappeared round the end of the building in search of the Chief.

Moments later, a white faced Senior Company Officer Moate came striding rapidly towards the front of the limousine with an equally white faced Buck hard on his heels. 'Why didn't you bloody-well check to see the safety pin was in position before you left?' he roared, as he headed for the rear of the vehicle. He stood back speechless for a moment, his eyes taking in the battered and twisted rear end of his beloved fire engine.

Then he exploded with anger and there followed the most distressing ten minutes of my life as the enraged officer swore and cursed the unfortunate Fireman Jones before turning on his heel and striding rapidly away in search of the unfortunate driver who had removed the vehicle from the Appliance House that morning and first connected the pump.

Several days were to elapse before poor Buck recovered from his ordeal. He never forgave the Chief for what he considered was an unfair accusation, maintaining that the vehicle was on 'Standby' ready for immediate call out when he took it over, and therefore the person really responsible for the accident was the duty driver.

A few weeks later an even greater tragedy was to overtake the station — the loss of the Selby Fire Boat. She was moored on the local canal, the responsibility of her skipper, Leading-fireman Billy Bean, ably assisted by a fulltime crew of one — in the shape of Fireman Bill Wright.

The fireboat enjoyed the proportions and appearance of a small barge, but hidden below her tiny decks were a couple of heavy duty firepumps mounted on massive concrete bases and driven by two gleaming Rolls Royce engines. Motive power provided by a small 8 hp marine engine gave the bluff-bowed vessel an impressive top speed of 5 knots! The Crew's living quarters were cramped, but comfortable, and it was clear that the two 'Bills' were both proud and fond of their little craft.

I looked forward with great eagerness to my occasional visits to the fire-boat. Here I was taught to scull a dinghy with a single oar over the transom and thanks to Bill Wright my knowledge of things maritime was extended and my use of knots and lashings improved.

One fine sunny June afternoon I was detailed to attend the fireboat for what today would be termed 'work experience'. Arriving at the boat I was delighted to learn that a short cruise along the canal was about to take place. 'To give the engine and pumps an airing' commented Leading-fireman Bean. For the best part of half an hour we chugged happily along the motionless canal to the open countryside beyond, my thoughts drifting lazily back to a childhood world with its 'Wind in the Willows' and the fascinating adventures of Toad, Rat, and Mole.

The command 'Take the stern painter and moor up' from the skipper brought me back to reality as engines started to throb below. For some fifteen minutes the little craft vibrated merrily as her powerful pumps forced six crackling jets of water high into the sky above our heads.

On the homeward run I was allowed to take the wheel, expressing youthful disappointment at the boat's snail-like performance. Having lived most of my life beside the Ouse, I was better acquainted than most with the dangers of this fast-flowing river. I asked Leading-fireman Bean how he would respond to a fire call from the O.C.O. Feed Mills down river with a spring tide running in the opposite direction?

'Report sick or wait until the bloody tide turns' came his terse and humourless reply, as I caught a belated shake of the head and a grimace from Fireman Wright in the corner of the boat's cockpit. It was only to be a matter of weeks before the truth of this seemingly frivolous statement would seal the fate of the game little fireboat.

On the Sunday morning in question, Senior Company Officer Moate had decided that, in the absence of the fireboat's skipper, he would personally conduct the exercise with her part-time crew.

A surprised and incredulous Lock-keeper penned the vessel through the lock and into the fast-flowing river with the Chief at the helm. As the little boat attempted to 'go about' she caught the full force of the tide, the power from her engine failing to counter the strength of the water and she began to drift helplessly upstream towards the nearby bridge.

Moments later she hit a bridge buttress broadside on and began to list dangerously as the powerful current pinioned her to the timbers. Her startled crew scrambled to safety onto the nearby buttress as the relentless pressure of the fast-flowing tide forced one of her gunwales below the surface and she slowly began to fill with water.

Heavily waterlogged, she refused to sink but as the tide slackened with the approach of high water, she slid quietly from view beneath the surface of the river.

We found her the following morning holed and forlorn, lying just below the bridge close to the Selby bank, stranded by the outgoing tide. Once again the luckless team of Jones and Booth were called upon and given the task of pumping her out.

'Heavily waterlogged, she refused to sink . . .'

A few days later we waved our farewells as a snappy little tug arrived from Goole to return her to her native port, there to be salvaged and scrapped.

*　　　*　　　*　　　*　　　*

British superstition inclines to the view that misfortune arrives in threes and Senior Company Officer Moate was soon to be involved in yet another mishap except that on this occasion his quick thinking was to save my life and at the same time contribute to the eventual loss of his officer status. For several months I had persisted with my request to be allowed to climb the Merryweather Turntable Ladder on its now frequent visits from Goole. Finally the Chief sought the advice of Column Officer Bailey — 'At his age Bob, I can't possibly give permission for him to work on the ladder' said the Column Officer. Then, smiling broadly, he winked and said 'but I could perhaps turn a blind eye'.

The Chief beckoned me to one side. 'I can't afford to let you break your bloody neck in front of all these people', he announced, as he eyed the crowded park benches, 'so listen carefully to what I have to say. I am going to climb first and when I reach the top, the Section Leader will send you up. Climb steadily as you have been taught, left arm, left leg, right arm, right leg — and don't let me see you letting go one rung before your other hand has gripped the next.' He paused for breath, sniffed and continued. 'Don't look down when you are climbing and don't be afraid to stop for a wind' and, turning on his heel, he strode briskly over to the Escape and began to climb with a speed and agility that would not have disgraced someone half his age.

My eyes followed his rapid progress up the ladder. On reaching the top he produced his precious pipe and matches and, with elbows resting on one of the rungs, proceeded to light his pipe as he gazed out thoughtfully over the Selby landscape.

'Good luck!' exclaimed Section Leader Vickerman as he signalled me aboard the platform of the ladder to start my climb. I was now feeling a little scared, almost wishing I had never mentioned the idea in the first place, for

the ladies of the Control Room were already occupying
their ringside seats — thank goodness Pauline was off
duty for I was not at all certain that I was going to have
the courage necessary to reach the top!

At first, the climb was fairly easy, the width of the
ladder and its massive construction providing a feeling of
confidence and security. As I continued climbing, its
width began to reduce alarmingly and the construction
seemed far less robust, the guard rails at either side now
almost brushing my shoulders.

I was becoming breathless, my mouth was dry and I
was feeling very frightened. I must be nearing the top;
better stop for a breather and attempt to calm my shattered nerves. Gripping the ladder firmly with both hands,
I stopped climbing and decided to take a quick look
upstairs.

Oh, no; despair overtook me. Apart from the section I
was negotiating, there were two more ahead, the last one
looking so distant and fragile that I marvelled it had not
buckled under the Chief's weight.

Then came a friendly voice from above 'Well done lad!
Take your time and don't be afraid to stop for another
wind', the Chief said encouragingly. With a considerable
effort of will I forced myself to continue the climb, star-
ing straight ahead, the whiteness of my knuckles as they
gripped each rung reflecting my determination and fear. I
hung onto each rung as if my life depended on it —
which of course it probably did. Then, after what seemed
an eternity, my eyes caught sight of the Chief's fireboots
just above me on the ladder — I had made it!

Gasping for breath, heart pounding like a steam hammer, I stopped and, taking a firm grip on the ladder,
looked upwards at the Chief's bulky figure. 'Get your
breath back lad, and then have a look at the view', he
said easily. I peered out cautiously through the ladder at
the majesty of Selby's ancient Norman Abbey that lay just
outside the Park to our right, the surrounding streets and
buildings now distant and remote, as if I was looking in
on them from another world.

'Come up a couple of treads and kick the pawl down
near your right foot and it will release a platform for you
to stand on', ordered the Chief. Despite a great effort of

will both feet refused to budge. 'I'm sorry Chief but I can't seem to lift either of my feet', I stammered lamely. He laughed. 'Don't worry lad! I've known firemen who've had far worse than sticking feet the first time up a Merryweather — some even manage to fill their rubber boots and I don't need to tell you what with'.

He chuckled, and began to describe landmarks and various other features in the town and countryside below, the giant ladder swaying gently in the still air of the warm afternoon. 'Right, Messenger Booth, that's enough for one day!' he suddenly exclaimed. 'Take care and remember that most people fall off ladders going down — not climbing them'.

Several times during the descent I found it necessary to check my speed, the return climb providing a pleasant end to the proceedings, and demanding very little in the way of physical effort and none of the tension and fear I felt on the way up.

I made several sorties up the ladder in the weeks that followed, my confidence growing with each new climb. Then came the day when Column Officer Bailey demonstrated the hair-raising feat of being lowered from the top of the Escape by a Davy line. For this exhilarating little exercise the descending crewman flings himself off the ladder, wearing a special safety harness attached to a line, his descent controlled by the winchman on the ground below.

The feat of rolling off the top of the Escape attached only to what appeared to me to be a very flimsy rope seemed a certain way of qualifying either for a high-wire act with a circus or immediate admission to the nearest mental institution. Not surprisingly, I declined the Chief's offer to take part in the spectacle but, by the end of the afternoon with the rest of the duty crew looking none the worse for the experience, I relented and was soon descending earthwards with a lack of concern that surprised me.

Three weeks and two 'drops' later I decided that my prowess on the Escape should be recorded for posterity and Bill Wright (of fireboat fame) agreed to take a photograph during the descent. I made a rapid ascent of the ladder, kicking down the platform pawl and standing

impatiently as the Chief attached the heavy spring clip of
the line to my safety harness. He straightened up. 'Alright
lad', he said, which I took as the command to go and
promptly rolled off the ladder to the accompaniment of a
shout of 'Hold it' from below!

I swung gently beneath the ladder and looking up saw
the Chief's anxious face peering down at me. Clearly
something had gone badly wrong. 'Shall I try to swing
onto the underside of the ladder Chief?' I suggested,
grateful still to be at the top of the ladder and not the
bottom. 'You keep bloody still. I've got you', rasped the
Chief, the veins standing out on his forehead. I cautiously
lowered my eyes, not daring to move, and saw a flurry of
activity below.

Whilst I had been climbing the winchman had been
explaining to a group of schoolchildren how the mechanism worked and had failed to secure the rope on his
winch. As a result I was now dangling in space, held
there by the quick reflexes and strength of Senior Company Officer Moate. 'You will have to winch him up
before you start to lower; my hands are trapped!' roared
the Chief at the unfortunate winchman below. Then after
what seemed an age I gently felt myself being inched
upwards and the Chief retrieved his bruised and bleeding
hands.

I descended safely, my camera returned by an ashen-
faced Bill Wright. 'Did you manage to get a picture Bill?'
I asked lightheartedly. 'My God John, if you had seen
things from down here I doubt whether you would be so
casual', he said and, thrusting the camera into my hands,
walked quickly away.

From his vantage point at the top of the ladder the
Chief now began to lambast the unfortunate winchman
below. His swearing outburst lasted for the best part of
five minutes, the unfortunate occupants of the nearby
park benches rising to their feet in horror and
amazement.

Nannies covered the ears of babies in prams and there
was a startled exodus of people from the area; clearly the
man on the fire escape had taken leave of his senses —
and had they but realised — for the best possible reasons.

'I swung gently beneath the ladder and looking up saw the Chief's anxious face peering down at me.'

61

Shortly afterwards I left Selby and its Fire Service to train full-time as an Observer with the Royal Observer Corps. 'I think you may find this a bit more exciting than the fire brigade', an enthusiastic Head Observer told me!

Months later, I heard the Chief had paid the price for the station's previous misfortunes which had culminated with his unfortunate outburst on the Merryweather Escape. It seems he was reported by a word-perfect member of the great British public who even managed to write down a list of the expletives he had used. A subsequent enquiry resulted in the loss of officer status, this hard-swearing but highly experienced and courageous Fire Officer reverting to the rank of Section Leader.

I last visited the Chief in 1975, then well into his eighties but still with that mischievious twinkle in his eyes. He was to die the following year, even as he told me he would, with his brave act remaining unrecognised, either by the community, or the Service he loved and served so well.

Death in the Orchard

Early one evening in the spring of 1943 a series of violent explosions shook Bridge House. Moments later father rushed in with the words 'I didn't hear the siren but I think they have bombed Kelfield'. I followed him outside into the darkness and saw the frightening glare of a large fire that certainly looked as if it was from Kelfield village some three miles distant.

(At this time German bombers were still attacking isolated targets in the North East although most of their recent efforts had been concentrating on the port and city of Hull some forty miles down river, which resulted in almost nightly 'alerts' in our district.)

Grabbing respirator and steel helmet I cycled rapidly along the High Street in the direction of the local Fire Station. Our wartime village fire brigade consisted of some ten or a dozen volunteers who met in a disused house in the centre of the village. The equipment included a Standard Gwynne medium trailer pump, towed by a somewhat elderly American Pontiac Saloon. The car was fitted with a rack that carried a forty foot extending ladder. A large brass bell fitted outboard near the front passenger seat completed the modifications and gave the turn-out the appearance of something belonging to an 'up-market' window cleaner!

On reaching the yard where the appliance was kept I was greeted with a, 'Well done lad, go round and get the crew out', from Leading Fireman Aubrey Kettlewood who lived nearby. He was already checking the gear on the trailer pump and I could tell from his manner that nothing was going to stop this, his first official turnout in nearly four years of war!

63

'. . . and gave the turnout the appearance of something belonging to an "up-market" window cleaner!'

Needing no second bidding I rode furiously along Sherburn Street to the nearby homes of the remaining members of the crew. In a matter of minutes I had made three calls. At each call, wives answered my urgent knocking and I panted out my message that their menfolk were urgently required at the appliance house in readiness for a fire-call. At the first two homes I was told that hubby wasn't very well and wouldn't be going. The remaining crewman had gone to bed, said his wife, and it would take too long to get him up. I looked up towards the bedroom window and I turned disappointedly away just in time to see a head complete with cap disappear behind the curtains!

It was whilst riding back to the station that I realized that the wives had all displayed considerable apprehension, if not fear, at the thought of their menfolk turning out for what they considered was clearly a dangerous assignment. The glow in the sky now seemed even more ominous and I recollect returning to the station somewhat lacking in the enthusiasm I had when leaving it some ten minutes earlier.

When told of the failure of my mission, Leading Fireman Kettlewood was furious. He had already started and run up the trailer pump and was standing near the Pontiac's masked headlamps with the engine running. I hope here, I may be forgiven for mentioning his rather unfortunate affliction. When he became angry or excited, a slight stutter became worse and one of his feet would start tapping the floor as if beating time to a quick-step. 'Bugger them', Aubrey said, his foot tapping wildly, 'we'll go on our bloody own', and we climbed hastily aboard the Pontiac and pulled out into the main street just as Aubrey spotted a local, 'Bosser' Elcock, who had spent some time with us as a volunteer fireman before transferring to Heavy Rescue. Aubrey quickly explained our predicament, 'Bosser' sprang into the car with us and we were off.

With firebell clanging loudly Aubrey made the fastest time down Cawood High Street of anyone before or since. We raced over the bridge with the car's speedometer registering 55 mph as the powerful Pontiac continued to gather speed. On the bridge, father was heard to comment to a bystander 'By God, Selby has been quick', not realising that the fire engine was the village firepump with his sixteen-year-old son ringing the bell.

As locals will know, the Ferry Lane is a dead straight section of highway, exactly a mile in length, which we covered at break-neck speed. Reaching the end of the lane, Aubrey turned right in the direction of Kelfield, having the same distance to travel before reaching the outskirts of the village. As we arrived at the scene, flames from the disaster lit the surrounding countryside like daylight and we quickly realised that we were not witnessing the results of German bombs.

In a large tree nearby hung the lifeless body of an airman entangled amidst the lines and canopy of a parachute. 'It's a bloody plane' gasped Aubrey, 'Where's the nearest water?' I knew the locality well from youthful bird-nesting expeditions. 'There's a large duckpond just through a gate a bit further on', I replied. 'That's a bit bloody close; where's the gate?' enquired Aubrey. The gate had already gone and was in use by a party of four or five villagers who were reverently carrying the prostrate body of another member of the aircraft's crew towards a nearby house.

Aubrey drove into the field and roared across the turf in the direction of the pond with the trailer jumping wildly behind us. We quickly manhandled the pump into position and started to connect up the heavy lengths of suction hose that fed water to the pump. One end was fitted with a strainer covered by a large wicker basket that prevented leaves and other debris being sucked into the pump.

Dragging the heavy basket towards the water I realised that I had insufficient hose to allow the basket to submerge. 'The basket's not covered!' I yelled, tugging madly at the hose. As I did so, Aubrey released a section that had fouled on one of the trailer pump wheels — just as I gave another frantic heave — and fell over backwards into the pond. As I scrambled to my feet in the foul smelling water Aubrey wryly commented, 'I don't know which is the greater hazard, the smell of you or the fire!'

My unfortunate ducking had clearly reduced my adrenalin supply and I was now very conscious of the sound of exploding ammunition (much too close for comfort) punctuated every now and then by deeper and more sinister explosions. 'John, run out the first length of hose. Bosser, you take the second and the branch', commanded Aubrey. With that, he swung the starting handle and the pump's engine roared into life. Grabbing a length of hose I thrust the coupling home on the delivery outlet of the pump and started off in the direction of the fire, unrolling the hose as I ran.

The route to the main blaze meant passing through a rather patchy hedge of blackthorn and in negotiating a slight incline I stumbled and fell over an obstruction. To my horror I discovered I'd fallen over the body of a man. In the light from the burning aircraft my impression was that he was black. I then realised I was looking at the badly burned body of yet another member of the aircraft's crew. Feeling sick and shocked I scrambled to my feet and continued running out the remainder of the hose. Bosser quickly caught me up passing without a word as I grabbed for the coupling on his hose length and joined the two together. I waited until I saw him snap home the branch-pipe and, running part way back to the pump, raised my arm for Aubrey to turn on the water. Almost at once, a powerful jet of water hit the flames and there was an immediate explosion that scattered burning debris in all directions.

I remembered thinking — all we need now is an air-raid. Surely the Germans will see the flames and thinking one of their aircraft had found a target will proceed to provide a further contribution. Meanwhile, the harder Bosser hit the blazing aircraft with his powerful water jet, the brighter the fire burned. Magnesium alloy or similar material on one of the aircraft's giant wheel hubs appeared to be the main source of the trouble and I rushed back to Aubrey on the pump with the information. 'We shall have to use the diffuser', said Aubrey decisively, 'I will give you a minute to reach Bosser and will then shut down the pump to allow him to change over'.

I dashed back with the replacement branchpipe and Bosser quickly changed over and immediately signalled his appreciation. Although the fine spray of the diffuser was much less effective than the foam our full-time crews at Selby used on aircraft fires, it was proving much more effective in damping down the fire than the jet from the original branchpipe.

Reporting back to Aubrey at the pump, I was surprised to find that the area was now milling with people. Many wearing the dark blue uniforms of the ARP and Rescue Services were moving about on the fringe of the disaster area.

It now transpired that Leading Fireman Kettlewood was becoming concerned about a possible shortage of petrol for the pump. Could I go over to the nearby farm in an attempt to obtain more fuel? On the way, I ventured a closer look at the dead airman, and was surprised to see that the body had been turned over, revealing a ring of white flesh around one wrist. Whilst we had been busy with the fire someone had been callous enough to steal the dead airman's watch.

I met someone near the farm building and asked where I might find the owner — 'Yes, he was the owner and what did I want?. I explained we were running low on petrol for the fire pump; could he help?' He led me to an outbuilding, a sort of granary and there, lying quietly on a pile of sacks, were the three or four surviving members of the bomber's crew. Though none of my business, I waited until we were out of earshot before asking why the survivors had not been taken indoors. It appeared that the lady of the house 'did not want the mess'.

As we walked away with me clutching the precious two-gallon can of petrol he asked if we could damp down his nearby corn stacks as he was afraid they would soon catch fire. Angered by the apparent callous treatment afforded to the surviving members of the aircraft's crew, I retorted 'It will serve you right if the bloody lot burns down'. I recollect that my indignant outburst worried me for weeks after the incident even more than the harrowing scenes I had witnessed that night. The man was an influential local farmer who knew father but fortunately did not realize who I was. Nonetheless, had father found out about his sixteen-year-old son's rudeness, I was in no doubt that the necessary apology would have to be made. Father never subscribed to the view that circumstances can sometimes alter cases!

Arriving back at the pump with the precious petrol I was staggered to see there wasn't a living soul in sight apart from Aubrey on the pump. 'Where has everyone gone?' I asked. 'They reckon she's got bombs on', said Aubrey philosophically. 'Well, what are we going to do?' I demanded, feeling that I at any rate still had a lot of living to do. 'Go and tell Bosser. I can't leave the pump', said Aubrey. To my shame, I took this to mean that Aubrey thought that two lengths of hose between himself and the stricken aircraft would ensure his continued survival if the bombs went off! I retorted, 'Well if she goes up, so will you'.

On my way back to Bosser, I skirted the debris looking for some tell-tale signs of the aircraft's identity. Certainly she was armed for ammunition for her Browning machine guns had been exploding since our arrival at the scene. Then my spirits rose — there on the broken aft section of the fuselage were the large squadron markings TT and I knew that all the Halifax bombers flying from nearby Riccall carried the squadron markings ZB or TT and Riccall was non-operational — a training station. With spirits rising I took over from Bosser on the branchpipe. He wanted to get home for they would be wondering where he was. Forty years on, I wonder whether anyone ever thanked him for his courage and unselfish efforts that night in a Kelfield orchard.

About half an hour later a quiet voice at my elbow said 'I'll take over now son', and a uniformed fireman took the branchpipe from my hands. With that a loud voice boomed 'Messenger Booth what the bloody hell are you doing here?' and striding towards us came the burly figure of Senior Company Officer Robert Moate. 'What crew have you got?' he demanded angrily 'One and a half sir. Leading Fireman Kettlewood and myself', 'You had no bloody business to turn out without my orders and never without a full crew', he replied, the annoyance registering in his voice. Then, putting his hand on my shoulder, he quietly said 'Well done lad. Don't come in tomorrow. Get off home now or your Mother will be worried as it's well past 2 o'clock'.

Before returning to the pump I decided to have a quick look around the village. Threading my way between the fallen electric cables and telephone wires, I was amazed to see that the Halifax had come down on the main street of the village, shedding engines and breaking up in the process as it skidded along the street. Where there was a gap between the houses, the bomber seemed miraculously to have taken it. One of its engines was imbedded in a wall within three feet of a nearby house and although we had tackled the main blaze, other firecrews from Selby had also been hard at work higher up in the village.

There are those who believe in miracles and those who

do not. How the villagers of Kelfield escaped death that night was little short of miraculous.

I visited the disaster the following day and a kindly local, unaware of my involvement the previous night, showed me where the aircraft had first hit a clump of tall trees on the outskirts of the village, knocking off the chimney pots of several houses as it crossed and re-crossed the street before finally coming to rest in the orchard of the farm.

Some weeks later our firemen attended a lecture given by an RAF officer on how to approach crashed aircraft and the position of emergency exits and cutting gear. Would we also exercise vigilance as far as the public were concerned and keep them well back for their own safety.

It was he said, a cause for regret that on one crash in the area recently, a gold wrist watch had been removed from the body of one of the crew. It had been a 21st birthday present from the boy's parents given to him a few weeks previously, a memento they would have treasured for the rest of their lives.

The Plotters — or a Spitfire for Breakfast

On a quiet Sunday morning early in May, 1944, Royal Observer Post King 4 lay quiet and still in the morning sunshine. Apart from a solitary Spitfire that had taken off from nearby Church Fenton on the regular Tyne-Tees patrol, none of the remaining posts in the circuit were plotting. 'It's bloody quiet this morning', commented Observer Wally Lazenby as he deftly dropped two eggs into a battered saucepan that was bubbling merrily on the post's tiny combustion stove. 'Here comes Billy with the milk', I replied from my vantage point on top of the old beer crate which assisted visibility on cold mornings without our having to drop the glass side-screens that surrounded the plotting table.

Billy was our local landlord, the post being located in one of the fields a short distance from his farmhouse. On weekdays we collected our own milk from his wife, but on Sunday mornings he would usually stroll over to the post, the visit often coinciding with one of his duty spells as a part-time observer.

After the usual greetings had been exchanged, Billy commented that he had a message from the Head Observer, Bert Pollard. 'He wants to see you before you go off at eleven, but he might be a few minutes late so don't go rushing off as it's important'. 'What's it about?' asked Wally with a trace of apprehension in his voice. 'He didn't say and I didn't ask', said Billy with his usual display of reticence. He climbed aboard the beer crate as I handed over my head-set and prepared myself for yet another breakfast encounter with one of Wally's hard boiled eggs!

Shortly before eleven, the Head Observer's car was spotted, heading along the Ferry Lane in the direction of the post. 'Good God', said Wally peering through the field glasses, 'he's in uniform and he's got Jim Hardgraves with him', 'Blimey, he's in uniform as well. I'll bet his chickens have gone without their breakfast this morning'. The Deputy Head Observer was a man of many parts, his various responsibilities including aircraft recognition, erratic spells as our village cobbler, and more recently the role of part-time chicken farmer! The official party drew to a halt on the hard standing opposite the post, their entry greeted with two steaming mugs of tea.

The Head Observer lost no time in coming to the point of the visit. 'Jim has picked our best six observers for a special recognition test next Sunday evening at The Anchor Inn with an Observer Officer from York Headquarters and as you two are on the list is there any reason why either of you can't attend?' Wally looked pensive for a moment. 'What sort of a test is it, Bert, and why?' he enquired mildly. 'All I can tell you is we shall be using combat film not cards. The rest you will know on Sunday night if you are chosen', said Bert importantly. The official party then left as quickly as it had arrived, no doubt to visit and inform the remaining observers of their duty to King 4 and country the following Sunday evening.

'It must be important. Bert seemed pretty serious about it', I commented to Wally as the Chief Whip and his deputy climbed aboard their car. 'Don't you believe it', said Wally, 'I expect he's had a bet with one of his cronies in York Centre about which post has the best observers and he'll look a bit bloody silly if none of us turn up to take part'.

On the following Sunday evening, six uniformed observers arrived at The Anchor Inn as directed to find the bar crowded with locals, several of the resident military, and a party of Air Force lads from nearby Church Fenton, the local fighter station. To our surprise there was no sign of the Head Observer, his deputy, or for that matter, the promised Observer Officer from York. Frank, the landlord, himself a part-time observer, leaned quietly over the bar. 'They are waiting for you in the back room', he whispered. 'They have got the door locked so you will need to knock'. 'Have we got to roll up our trouser legs?' asked Wally, a somewhat strange remark that appeared to pass unnoticed as the party trooped out of the bar.

Wally knocked loudly on the door and we were ushered into the presence of the missing trio who were sharing the room with a large cine projector and the screen that instructor Jim Hardgraves normally used for projecting aircraft silhouettes on his epidiascope. The Head Observer introduced the mysterious visitor who explained that we were to take part in a special aircraft recognition test. Pencils and paper were handed round and for the best part of an hour we furiously scribbled as a variety of aircraft flashed across the screen, sometimes exploding before we had time to decide whether they were British or German.

'. . . as a variety of aircraft flashed across the screen, sometimes exploding before we had time to decide whether they were British or German.'

73

The test ended and the papers were rapidly collected. 'There's a drink for you all at the bar', announced the Head Observer magnanimously, 'but don't leave just yet. We might want another word with one or two of you'. The party lost no time in repairing to the bar to find that numbers had thinned somewhat apart from a sprinkling of Air Force uniforms. I was on the point of sampling a small shandy when Instructor Hardgraves appeared at my elbow. 'John, we would like a word with you', he said.

The Observer Officer from York was looking pensive. 'How old are you John?' he asked. 'Nearly seventeen and a half sir'. 'You know you have signed the Official Secrets Act and therefore anything I say to you must not be repeated to anyone, including your parents'. 'Yes sir', I replied 'Have you any idea why you were all called in to take part in this test this evening?' he asked. Suddenly Wally's explanation for the test being held seemed a little flimsy, so I decided against venturing an opinion. The Observer Officer lowered his voice to a whisper and then dropped his bombshell. 'Within the next few weeks we are going to invade Europe', he said, 'and my job is to recruit personnel from the Royal Observer Corps who will take part by assisting the gunnery officers on board the Naval support vessels. You scored 89 out of a possible hundred on tonight's test but sadly none of your colleagues managed better than 45. I am prepared to put your name forward when you have had a little time to think the matter over'.

'Are there any questions you would like to ask me?' he enquired kindly. 'Yes sir, don't the Navy have their own observers?' 'Well, they do but in the heat of the moment they have sometimes fired on and even shot down our own aircraft in the past. The practice is by no means confined to the Navy for it has happened with the RAF as well. All aircraft taking part in the invasion will be carrying special markings. I can't tell you any more about that just at the moment but you will hear in due course and it should help'.

I left the interview in a daze and returned to the bar to find Wally Lazenby in conversation with a familiar face, Sergeant Douthwaite, one of Roger Richardson's old fighter pilot friends who had recently returned from the

Middle East with his Squadron and was now displaying the narrow braid of a Pilot Officer. 'Yes, he was back at good old Church Fenton and, no, as far as he knew he had not shot down any 'Jerries' whilst he was in the Middle East', he said. Wally was busily explaining to him our role as observers at King 4. 'Oh yes, nothing happened in the air around Church Fenton that we didn't know about' said Wally. I shall be on patrol in the morning at 7' announced Pilot Officer Douthwaite. 'Good' remarked Wally, 'pop in for a cup of tea. We shall be on duty from 7 a.m. and if you are airborne a bit early I expect you will see John on his motor cycle and sidecar breaking the speed limit along Ferry Lane at about five to seven'.

I took little account of the conversation, my mind being too full of the implications and excitement of perhaps taking part in the forthcoming seaborne invasion of Europe.

Monday morning was bright and sunny and the 500cc Enfield coughed a couple of times and spluttered into life. I threw my respirator and steel helmet into the sidecar and we were off. The Enfield was a side valve, not particularly fast and somewhat noisy. With luck I could manage about 55 mph along the lane before having to shut down. With the previous evening's prospects very much in mind I left in a light-hearted mood and decided that this morning I would really set up a new record for the mile-long stretch of the Ferry Lane.

I acknowledged a friendly wave from father as I crossed the bridge, opening the throttle wide and leaning forward and low over the Enfield's squarish tank as we roared down the lane in the direction of the post. The spring grass at either side of the road had already reached a height of several feet and I decided that if I left the road it would perhaps help to cushion my fall.

Suddenly I saw the surrounding grass flatten and at the same time heard a roar that drowned the Enfield's noisy beat as Mr Douthwaite's Spitfire nearly took my head off, causing me to almost lose control of the bike as he rocketed along the Ferry Lane at zero feet! Somewhat white and shaken, I reached the post to find Wally, who had just arrived on his cycle and had seen the incident, in near hysterics. 'I told you he was calling in for a cup of tea', laughed Wally, as he rushed off in the direction of the post.

Meanwhile, the Spitfire had climbed to some five hundred feet and was circuiting back towards the village. He came over the post as if to establish that we were there, banked, and once again flew over Cawood. By this time I was watching him through the glasses and I commented to Wally that he was losing height, obviously intent on 'buzzing' us, whereupon Observer Lazenby climbed up on the outside bank brandishing a broom in one hand and a mug in the other.

I lost the Spitfire for a few moments and then saw it lifting gently to clear the low hedges of nearby fields as it raced towards the post almost at ground level. Wally appeared to be quite oblivious of the danger to his position as it roared across the adjoining fields, for I was now looking down on the plane with my field glasses from my vantage point inside the post. 'For God's sake get down Wally', I yelled as the aircraft roared towards us, but Wally continued to stand his ground. Suddenly, with the Spitfire less than a hundred yards away, either his courage failed or Wally decided that discretion was the better part of valour and he dived headlong into the post, his arm colliding with the edge of the plotting table on his downward descent.

For several weeks after the incident, Observer Lazenby had the tricky task of riding to work with one arm in a sling, his unfortunate fall having fractured his arm. Being something of a gentleman he explained his indisposition in a variety of ways, none of which took account of the fact that he had invited — and nearly received — a Spitfire for breakfast!

'. . . Observer Lazenby had the tricky task of riding to work with one arm in a sling . . .'

One of our aircraft failed to return. . . .

If the reader had been standing outside Cawood Police Station early one morning in the Spring of 1944 he would have witnessed a most extraordinary sight and one which would have convinced the enemy that whilst our aircraft were not running short of bombs, our airmen appeared to be running short of clothing!

As I recollect, the gentleman in question was dressed in Royal Air Force uniform, wearing sergeant's stripes and the insignia of a Wireless Operator/Air Gunner which was an indication that he was above average intelligence in that he was able to transmit and receive wireless messages whilst at the same time engaging in the task of shooting down enemy aircraft with his Browning machine guns!

He was however improperly dressed, being minus his hat and one flying boot; no doubt the Station Warrant Officer would be anxious to know in due course why these items of clothing were littering the Yorkshire countryside.

It is possible, that, had all the incriminating evidence been available at the time instead of forty-one years later, he and his colleagues might have been charged with a rather more serious offence — that of bombing the county of Yorkshire with a Lancaster bomber!

On the previous evening your storyteller had reported for duty at Royal Observer Post King 4 at 23.00 hrs and was aware from an entry in the post logbook that a considerable number of aircraft had left earlier in the evening for foreign parts and were expected back for early bacon and eggs around 5 a.m. the following morning.

It was a fine clear night with little air activity. Around 1 a.m. one of our sister posts came in with a sound plot 'King 2, heard 15, west, angle 5', which meant Mr Hatfield the Head Observer, either had remarkable hearing, or had got the plot wrong! As he stopped speaking there was a series of loud explosions that lit up the skyline like daylight as the offending aircraft proceeded to bomb the Yorkshire Moors.

Quite naturally Mr. Hatfield regarded this as the action of an enemy aircraft and his second plot appeared to confirm this. 'King 2, Hostile overhead west'. A minute or so later he delivered his final plot. 'King 2, I am losing the hostile at 45 west, over to you King 4'. By simple deduction as we lay due west of King 2, it was not unreasonable to assume that in a few minutes we should have the offending hostile aircraft over us. I prayed he had got rid of all his bombs!

At this juncture, the young lady plotter at Group Headquarters in York was somewhat tactless. 'King 2 there are no hostile aircraft on the table at present' she insisted which rather suggested that either she didn't believe Mr Hatfield's story about the bombs, or alternatively one of our own aircraft was to blame. 'Are you trying to tell me that we are being bombed by one of our own bloody aircraft?' demanded Mr. Hatfield heatedly. It is of course, an offence to swear on the telephone, but I felt some sympathy for Mr Hatfield who had been rather closer to the offending stick of bombs than was the young lady at York Centre.

This quite reasonable question was countered by a firm repeat. 'All I can tell you King 2 is that 'home security' assure me there are no hostile aircraft over the north-east at the present time'. Here it is necessary to digress a little for 'home security' was a civilian gentleman who sat importantly in the Operations Room at Observer Headquarters charged with the difficult task of deciding whether to sound the Air Raid warning or not and perhaps more significantly — when to sound the All Clear!

In order to arrive at these weighty decisions he had to rely on a variety of outside agencies, including Fighter

Command, Bomber Command, the Air Ministry, the Home Secretary and sometimes in desperation, the various aircraft plots that appeared on the large map beneath him, provided by the illustrous Corps of which I was, at that time, a member.

I had now picked up the sound of the offending aircraft whose engines had the familiar ring of Rolls Royce Merlin's. I estimated its height at about 6,000 feet and deduced from its speed that it was not fast enough for a Mosquito — it had to be a Lancaster. For my first plot I made no mention of its possible country of origin for I was busily trying to waken my colleague Billy Appleyard who was remarkable on night sound plotting.

'I'm sorry to wake you Billy, but what's that overhead?' I demanded. He listened for a moment to the familiar note of the engines — 'Don't be bloody silly John, that's a Lanc. You know that as well as I do' and promptly went back to sleep. I took a deep breath; I was seventeen and about to range myself against the might and authority of the Head Observer at King 2. I blurted out my plot. 'King 4, heard, overheard west — this is a Lancaster on sound Centre'.

The Head Observer at King 2 exploded. 'You bloody fool, that's no Lancaster, you wouldn't be plotting the bastard as a Lancaster if you had been as close to his bombs as we were'. The minutes ticked by in silence; thank goodness I was losing the aircraft into Leeds area, still flying due west.

Here the saga might have ended except that the damned pilot decided at the last moment he wouldn't go to Leeds and turning round passed over us again, flying back due East. I had the unenviable task of passing him back to the Head Observer at King 2 who immediately reinstated his original plot as 'hostile'. The plotter in the Centre continued to receive a series of hostile plots from King 2 without further comment but the sirens hadn't sounded and I was certain the aircraft was a Lancaster.

The remainder of the night passed quietly and we were relieved at 7 am by Observers Hargraves and Price — the country couldn't be in better hands. Naturally they wanted to know all about the bombing but there was little we could tell them except that the target was in the general direction of King 2.

I had been offered a lift into Selby that morning by Roger (of Wager fame) providing I was at the farm by 9 a.m. sharp. As we were driving past the police station a few minutes later we were accosted by P.C. Wilkes with arm raised. Could we give a lift to an RAF lad who wanted to get to Wakefield asked P.C. Wilkes. 'Of course we can' said Roger with his usual bonhomie. P.C. Wilkes returned to the house and quickly reappeared with a tall young airman wearing a white fisherman's sock on one leg and a flying boot on the other, which is where I recollect this story started.

I vacated the co-pilot's seat in the front of the legendary Riley Sports and hopped in the back as Roger drove off quite unconcerned as if it was a common occurrence for him to transport bootless airmen about, for Roger was too much of a gentleman to ask why the passenger was wandering about minus a flying boot. I had no such inhibitions however, and our passenger might well be able to offer an explanation as to why Yorkshire needed to be bombed by a Lancaster.

I produced my Air Ministry Pass with its photograph of me that could easily have been mistaken for the Prime Minister of Japan. 'Was he,' I asked 'flying in this vicinity at around 2 a.m. this morning?' He smiled and nodded. 'Was he flying in a Lancaster bomber?' Again the affirmative nod. The next question caused confusion. 'Then why the blazes did you drop your bomb load on the East Riding of Yorkshire?' His smile had now disappeared and there was a distinct look of concern on his face. 'How the hell did you know that?' he asked tersely.

Roger had detected a crisis point in the conversation and proffered him a cigarette as he laughingly said 'I shouldn't answer any more questions if I were you, it might incriminate you. John does tend to take things rather seriously'. 'This was serious, Roger', I retorted. 'They nearly hit one of our posts, quite apart from the fact that the entire north east was nearly woken up with what would have proved to be a bogus Air Raid warning'.

'Look sergeant,' I continued somewhat more reasonably, 'we have all signed the Official Secrets Act and Mr Richardson is an officer in the Special Constabulary, so this conversation is unlikely to go further. May I recount my experiences on the post last night and you can fill in the missing bits, as my reputation could be on the line over this little lot!'

The sergeant listened patiently as I related the events of the previous evening and appeared astonished with the accurate information I was able to provide about the movements of the erring Lancaster. Then he told his story.

The Lancaster was one of a substantial force of bomber aircraft that had been dispatched to 'soften up' the German defences in Normandy and was the crew's last mission before the completion of their tour. En route to the target the aircraft developed serious faults to its electrical system which had affected the hydraulics on the aircraft. The bomb load was fused but the bomb doors refused to open. The skipper decided to abort the mission and return to base. Returning over the North Sea they had managed to open the bomb doors on the aircraft, but the bombs showed no desire to part company from the aircraft!

The skipper decided to fly inland to enable the crew to bale out before ditching the aircraft in the sea — a not unreasonable decision in view of all the circumstances. Then the engineer announced that the bomb release mechanism appeared to be working and after a quick look below, announced that they appeared to be over a remote region of the Yorkshire Moors. At this, the skipper gave the order for the bombs to be released, which led the Observer Corps to the quite understandable conclusion that they were an enemy aircraft.

Flying due west, the skipper gave the order for the crew to 'bale out' and had we but known at the time, the crew were all parachuting earthwards as they passed over Cawood. He then turned the aircraft back on an easterly course until he saw the coast appear below. The skipper baled out, and the Lancaster, now low on fuel, met a watery grave in the sea off Flamborough Head.

There were a number of mitigating circumstances for this drastic action explained the sergeant. The machine had taken a great deal of punishment during their tour, engines were due to be changed and there were clearly many problems with the aircraft that were bound to cause a lot of problems for the ground staff, even if they managed to sort them out. What's more the skipper didn't see why some other 'poor sods' should be expected to risk their lives in what was now — a clapped out crate. It would be better this way.

Roger had listened quite fascinated to the story as we drove towards Selby and was anxious to know whether he had any information about the fate of the rest of the crew. We were pleased to hear that the sergeant had telephoned his base earlier that morning and all the crew were safe and well apart from one who had broken his ankle on landing.

We dropped the sergeant at the bus stop in the Market Place at Selby and left him standing quietly in the queue to the curious glances of the waiting passengers who had quickly observed he was minus a flying boot. It would be a fitting end to the tale to know that the sergeant made it to the end of the war. Who knows, perhaps he is still living in Wakefield — one of the few Yorkshiremen that can claim to having bombed his own county in war!

*'We dropped the sergeant at the bus stop . . . standing
quietly in the queue to the curious glances of waiting
passengers . . .'*

Things that go bump in the night

The Royal Air Force station at Church Fenton was completed in the late 1930's and I recollect the short cut we youngsters used to take across the neighbouring fields to lie in the long grass surrounding the aerodrome as we watched the Gloster Gladiator and Hawker Demon biplanes practising their 'tricks' for the Opening Air Day. One Saturday Sir Kingsley Wood arrived to inspect the impressive line-up of silver four-engined De Haviland Biplanes with the bright red 'Airmail' lettering on their fuselages.

At the time of the Battle of Britain father said that the pilots came up to Church Fenton for a rest from the War in the south. To us children they always seemed to be resting, either sitting in deck-chairs or lying on the grass in their shirtsleeves and all wearing life-jackets. We thought this rather strange as there was no water for them to fall into at Church Fenton!

During the weeks leading up to the invasion of Europe there was considerable activity at Church Fenton the station having gone over to an offensive role with its Mosquito fighter bombers. Often they would journey south to Coltishall, there to 'bomb up' and re-fuel before departing for offensive operations against the Continent. The all wood 'Mossie' was a remarkable aeroplane powered by twin Rolls-Royce engines and carried a crew of two. In 1942 when it was first introduced it was considerably faster than any other aircraft in service with a maximum speed in the region of 400 mph.

To us children they always seemed to be resting . . .

Things that go bump in the night

There was then great activity above the Plain of York with Dakota and Stirling aircraft towing gliders south in readiness for the airborne landings in Normandy. On the day of our story, the weather was foul with a nasty fine penetrating rain that would quickly soak one to the skin without the protection of our famous 'Zeekee' coats. The Zeekee was standard issue in the Royal Observer Corps and was really three coats in one; a waterproof gaberdine outer, with oilskin beneath and an inner lining of woollen material.

Observer Sidney Price gazed around at the dismal weather and handed me his head-set. 'I'm off to see a man about a dog', he said, picking up the nearby coal scuttle as he ducked through the low doorway of the post and limped off down the path in the direction of the nearby coke-store. There was little going on in the air as the Observers on the three neighbouring posts complained to each other about the weather and chatted about nothing in particular.

'King 4' broke in the voice of the female plotter at Observer H.Q., 'Will you please look out for three Mosquito aircraft now leaving Church Fenton that are being "told" to Coltishall'? The expression 'Told' indicated that the aircraft were to receive priority as far as our plotting was concerned. They could be on a special operational mission, or perhaps carrying a VIP. Aircraft in distress were usually plotted in this manner. The instruction required that they be plotted on every square on the table of the grid, not every other one, as was usual in normal plotting.

'If they take off towards Leeds area I don't hold out much hope of seeing them Centre,' I said. 'We have ten-tenths cloud, poor visibility and low cloud base, possibly under 1,000 feet'. Sid had now returned and was listening intently for the familiar sound of the Mosquitoes engines. 'There's one of 'em' said Sid, pointing in the direction of Cawood village. The Mosquito was heading south, flying quite low, possibly under 500ft. I gave the Centre two rapid plots and he was gone.

A few minutes later, a second Mosquito appeared, quite a bit higher as he occasionally passed through wisps of cloud and rather nearer to us as he also headed south.

The minutes ticked by without a sign of the third aeroplane. 'I reckon he's given us the slip' said Sidney ruefully, just as the Centre plotter came on the air. 'King 4' she said urgently. 'Is there any sign of the third Mosquito as Church Fenton has lost radio contact?'

'He must have slipped through on the Leeds side Centre . . .' and then I stopped in mid-flow. 'Oh my God Centre, I've got him now and one of his engines is on fire!'.

The stricken Mosquito, unlike his two companions, must have made a right-hand circuit on take-off and was now heading towards the post with his port engine blazing furiously, leaving a trail of black smoke behind. He was losing height as he passed to the south of the post at about 800 feet.

'1 am connecting you with Church Fenton' said the plotter easily. There was a gentle click and a quiet male voice said 'Give me a running commentary on the aircraft's movements please King 4'. I changed from the normal plotting procedure as I described each manoevre made by the descending aircraft. The conversation could not have lasted more than a couple of minutes and I lost visual contact as the Mosquito disappeared behind the tree-line in the direction of nearby Riccall Aerodrome.

Almost at once there was a familiar mushroom of black smoke. 'Well that's that', said Sidney, 'I reckon they have bought it!'

'Oh I don't know though' Sidney reflected. 'They might have had time to get out' before she "brewed up".'

The following day I reported at 3 pm in the afternoon to find the deputy Head Observer Jim ('bun-guts') Hardgraves studying the post's logbook rather intently. Jim had an insatiable appetite for cakes, hence his unfortunate nickname. Mr. Hardgraves looked up from his reading, his glasses perched on the end of his nose. He chortled. 'Have a look in the logbook, Master Booth. The Royal Air Force have written some rude remarks about thee' he said, smiling.

The message was written in a bold clear hand in ink which caused it to stand out starkly against the usual pencilled scribble in the log. It said:-

'Why can't a couple of chaps have a quiet "brew-up" with their Mosquito without someone reporting their every move to base?'

Below were the signatures of the two intrepid airmen and beneath 'Best wishes to all the lads at King Four'.

My entry in the log covering the incident the previous day stated '. . . the aircraft appeared to fire on landing and it is unlikely that the crew could have survived'. Against this, written in the same bold hand, were three words 'But we did!' Church Fenton sent a car to Riccall to collect them and they called at the post only minutes after Sid and I had gone off duty. 'Fit as fleas and without a scratch' announced Observer Lazenby a day or so later.

The following week, we plotted a very similar incident involving a wing of Typhoon fighters. The aircraft were flying quite low, possibly under 500 feet, with the stern machine well behind and trailing smoke. 'Blimey' said Wally Lazenby ('Blimey' was Wally's favourite expression!) peering through the glasses 'This bugger's on fire an' all'. Within a matter of seconds the trailing aircraft suddenly banked and began to lose height. Wally was watching it intently through the field-glasses and saw the aircraft had lowered its undercarriage. Before disappearing behind distant trees. 'I reckon he's gone down into the Wharfe' said Wally, 'there's nowhere he could land there'. Sometime later the Centre plotter announced 'King 4, you will be pleased to hear that the Typhoon landed safely at Acaster Malbis.' 'Well I'm damned' said Wally 'I didn't even know there was an aerodrome there — it's nice to feel wanted. Put the kettle on lad — we'll celebrate!'

'King 4', said the Centre plotter with a certain urgency in her voice, 'Riccall appear to have lost one of their Halifax bombers!' It was 10 o'clock on a fine Saturday morning in July 1944 and since dawn the Halifax bombers from the nearby Heavy Conversion Unit had been practising 'circuits and bumps'. The machines would take off, make a circuit of the airfield and then proceed to land. After touch-down, throttles would be opened wide and the aircraft would again take off and resume their places in the circuit.

'One thing is certain', said Observer Sidney Price, as he rubbed his pipe stem reflectively against his chin, 'wherever he has gone down he hasn't fired or we should have seen him'. He eyed the circling Halifax bombers for a moment. 'I'll tell you what', said Sidney thoughtfully. 'If you have a ride down Cawood Inngs when you go off at eleven I reckon you will find that missing Halifax sitting quietly in a field.'

Sidney proceeded to elaborate. 'Look, they are taking off in this direction coming right over the post. Right!' I nodded. 'If they are the right way up and flying normally, we don't give 'em a second look. Right!' I nodded again. 'So,' said Sidney triumphantly, 'once they have passed the post we probably wouldn't be watching them.' He was now in full flight. 'I reckon he lost power just after take off and he's put the thing down over yon' bank in Cawood Inngs,' said Detective Price with great conviction.

Sidney's reasoning was sound. After all a Halifax bomber wasn't exactly the sort of thing that you could hide in somebody's back garden and, according to the plotter at York Centre, it had been missing for the best part of an hour. 'That's the only place within a five-mile radius of Riccall that could be isolated enough for him to land without anyone seeing him' reflected Sidney quietly, 'but I would have thought his mates could have seen him from the air.' 'Perhaps Riccall didn't like to ask them' I countered, 'just in case he's a bit mangled; it might upset them.'

At 11 o'clock precisely, Observer Lazenby joined us in the post and I left in some haste as the Royal Enfield combination roared off in the direction of Cawood Village. Mother had agreed the previous evening to provide a late breakfast when I came off at eleven. The least I could do would be to call and tell her I wouldn't be needing it.

'I am off to look for a crashed Halifax, Mother,' I explained, pausing briefly in the doorway. 'Oh, no you're not' insisted mother. 'I have cooked egg, bacon and fried bread and you are going to eat it!' I was about to remonstrate and then heard father's voice behind me — he was coming in from the bridge for his mid-morning drink. I ate my breakfast quickly with a hurried 'see you later' as I made for the door, the remains of the fried bread still in my hand. 'What's got into him this morning?' demanded father 'He's off to look for a crashed Halifax', explained mother despairingly, as I promptly closed the door and fled in the direction of the Royal Enfield.

The Inngs were a fairly extensive area of low ground lying close to the river that had been drained in previous centuries and now provided excellent farm land. They were somewhat remote from the village and the only inhabitants of the area were Frankie Firth and Maria who lived in a tiny hut with their two dogs. Frankie was a well known local character with features that very much resembled 'Old Bill', Bruce Bairnsfather's rustic character from World War One.

Frankie had great difficulty in walking and always employed two sticks being 'towed by a dog' tethered to each hand. The walk to the village on Friday evenings must have taken hours and it was rumoured that when Frankie returned later in the evening 'full of good cheer' he would sometimes break his journey by spending the night on a convenient hay stack, a practice strongly disapproved of by Maria!

My search of the Inngs had proved fruitless and I called on Frankie to ask whether he had seen anything of the missing bomber. 'Have you seen anything of an aeroplane on the ground around here? I asked. Frankie looked puzzled for a moment and I could tell from the resulting expression on his face that he was sure he was dealing with an idiot. 'What would anyone bring an aeryplane down here for?' he asked and, without waiting for a reply, promptly shut the door in my face!

I climbed back aboard the Royal Enfield and decided to return home after the best part of an hour's fruitless searching. In turning, I suddenly noticed the bent blades of several propellers sticking up over the hedge in a nearby field. Sidney had been right — the missing Halifax was here after all.

Leaving the motor cycle I walked across a nearby grass field and through a convenient gap in the hedge. There in the neighbouring field, her crew sitting on the tail smoking, was the bomber, completely surrounded by hedges on all sides and looking for all the world as if a giant hand had dropped it into the field.

As I approached, I could see where she had first touched down as her wheels ploughed two deep grooves in the soft ground. The tip of her starboard wing was missing where she had clipped a small tree but her undercarriage appeared intact. She still had her nose up and, apart from some bent propeller blades, was still very much in one piece.

Her crew appeared quite unconcerned about their lucky escape but for me this was the first Halifax I had been able to inspect at close quarters that was not in pieces. It seems the pilot-instructor of the aircraft had been at the controls when they got into difficulties, and he it was who had now set off in the direction of distant houses near the village of Wistow. 'He's been gone well over an hour' grumbled one of the crew, 'I reckon he's got himself bloody lost!'

The following day I decided to have one more look at the unfortunate aeroplane and jogged off down the Inngs on the motor cycle. To my surprise the 'Halibag' had gone! Apart from the deeply rutted field there was no evidence that an aircraft had ever been there.

RAF Riccall was to suffer even more excitement a few weeks later when a dozen or more American Flying Fortress bombers suddenly appeared from the south and started to circle the aerodrome. 'It looks as if the Americans are coming to Riccall' I commented to my Observer colleague as the giant machines began to quickly lose height. 'Bless me' said Instructor Hardgraves (who never used bad language) peering through the field glasses, 'they are all shot to pieces'. The machines passed overhead, some running on three engines, holes in wings and fuselages, and one with part of its tailplane missing. It was clear that all had taken terrible punishment wherever they had been.

The leading Fortress dropped from sight beneath the wood that bordered the airfield with a second close on his tail. I saw the red flare, warning the following aircraft not to land. Either the pilot did not see the flare, or he decided to ignore it and he too disappeared behind the tree line, quickly followed by the remainder of the flight.

For some fifteen minutes the sky over Riccall took on the appearance of a firework display as red flares continued to shoot skywards, all to be ignored by the descending bombers.

All apparently landed safely, quickly making for the grass perimeter to clear the runway for those following, only to come to grief in the soggy East Riding mud as they sank up to their axles in the soft ground. Hatches opened and uninjured crewmen waved frantically as ambulances sped towards the beleaguered aircraft.

'That must have been a terrible experience for them, poor lads' commented the deputy Head Observer as he made a bee-line for the post's logbook. 'And what about all those doodle-things that are landing down south? It looks to me as if it's a long way from being over yet' he said, consoling himself by sinking his teeth into one of his favourite buns.

We were together on the post some weeks later in early September when a distant vapour trail caught my eye. Jim was breakfasting in the little lean-to that adjoined the post and I had been watching the farmers in nearby fields as they loaded the last of the stooks of corn onto their farm carts. It was a beautifully clear morning with a cloudless sky and I was trying to come to terms with the fact that I had looked south only moments previously and that vapour trail wasn't there!

'Jim, come and have a look at this vapour trail' I invited, 'it seems to be going straight up'. The distant vapour trail was almost due south and dead vertical, its lower end out of sight on the skyline, its top high in the sky to the south of the post. 'Well I'm blessed' said Instructor Hardgraves, 'It can't be a plane; perhaps its one of them doodle-bug things.'

I gave my plot to the Centre at York. 'King 4, I have a vertical vapour trail at 27 degrees south.' 'Did you say a vertical vapour trail?' the plotter enquired incredulously. 'That's right Centre, it can't be a plane because it appears to be going up, rather than across the sky.'

'Can you get an angle on it for me, King 4?' I put the height bar of the instrument up to maximum altitude; I recollect it was somewhere in the region of 40,000ft and far higher than any aircraft we were ever likely to plot.

Try as I might, it was physically impossible to locate the top of the trail in the sighting device on the instrument. 'Centre, this is ridiculous. According to my instrument that vapour trail must be several hundred miles away, but how can one see that far?' The girl seemed relieved. 'Oh, well, never mind, King 4, it's well out of our area.' There was something about her tone of voice that led me to believe that she knew more about the incident than she was prepared to say.

Less than a week later, the Government announced that the Germans had introduced yet another terror weapon, the V2 rocket, much more deadly than the V1. This device gave no warning of its approach. The combined efforts of the Air Forces and advance of Allied troops had taken care of the doodle-bug menace. This had been replaced by something so terrible that Herbert Morrison, a senior Minister in the Government, had urged the War Cabinet to evacuate the entire population of the City of London!

I have won many bets over the years (and I'm not normally a betting man) from people who claimed that there were never any 'doodle-bugs' over north eastern England and Yorkshire in particular. In late September, 1944, one landed very close to Pocklington in the East Riding, something less than 25 miles from our own post.

I was on the headphones at King 4 when King 3 came in with a sound plot. 'I'm sure its an Auster, Centre, and he's flying very low and heading in the direction of the post.' The Observer at King 3 was so impressed by the Auster's low altitude that he let us all have a listen and the noise came over the earphones quite distinctly. 'Sounds more like a bloody motorboat than an aeroplane', commented old Chris at King 1. King 3 broke in. 'No wonder he's so low Centre; he appears to be on fire.'

'Oh dear,' said King 3 unhappily, 'his engine has cut but the fire seems to have gone out.' Seconds later there was a deafening explosion which I caught immediately over the headphones as I saw the distant flash of the missile light the horizon to the east. King 3 was still sure that what he had seen was an aircraft but was in some difficulty in reconciling this with the intensity of the explosion.

He had plotted a V1 and had not the device been heading straight for his post when he first picked it up on sound, he would no doubt have seen the blow-lamp glow from its rocket motor.

I was soon to join the Army and so had other things on my mind, so much so that I never really gave much thought to where the 'doodle-bug' had originated from. The thought did cross my mind at the time that it might have been a longer range weapon released from the Scandinavian coast. 'Not so,' said an RAF fighter pilot of my aquaintance who shared the same 'local' on occasions. 'The ones in the north east were released from Heinkel III bombers. I know because I used to have to go out at night and try to shoot the blasted things down before they got too far inland!'

It seemed to me at the time that this was quite a different war from the days of the old Whitleys and Hampdens and dear old Church Fenton's, Demons and Gladiators. It was all getting too scientific — perhaps the Army wouldn't be a bad choice after all . . . !

Off to War!

It was November 1944 and, said father optimistically, 'It looks as if it will be all over in Europe by Christmas'. The net was now closing on Germany with the Russians advancing from the East and Britain and her Allies from the West.

There was a knock on the door and the village post lady handed over a single buff envelope 'One from the King today Mr. Booth' she said as father accepted the letter marked O.H.M.S. and eyed it curiously. He thrust it in my direction 'It's for thee lad' he said.

The letter was brief and to the point. I was required to register at the local office of the Ministry of Labour and National Service on the date stated, pending a decision as to where my services could best be used in the national interest. I felt I had not done too badly up to now as far as 'the national interest' was concerned, but if the Minister wanted me down a mine with the rest of his Bevin Boys, there was little I could do about the matter.

It appeared these weighty issues would be decided after a visit to Doncaster and on the duly appointed day I climbed aboard the bus in Selby wearing my best suit and feeling somewhat unenthusiastic about the whole idea.

The Reception Centre was in an old school and I handed in my card on arrival and was told to wait, which in the circumstances, seemed a rather needless request. I eyed my fellow sufferers in the waiting room, all of whom sat silent and glum as they doubtless contemplated the respective merits of digging coal or shooting Japanese, for this alternative was clearly on the cards once the war in Europe had ended.

We were summoned to appear in alphabetical order by a civilian clerk who was distressed to find that most of his customers whose names began with 'A' had failed to attend. This was fortunate for the 'B's' and I was handed a form with my name at the top and ordered to proceed.

I entered a room that was very large and very cold, despite the glow from a small combustion stove at its centre. Here, some half a dozen elderly gentlemen appeared to be attempting to hide themselves behind a variety of portable hessian screens. A couple were wearing stethoscopes around their necks and the remainder were supported by various bits of equipment including scales, a device for measuring height, and a board with letters of the alphabet arranged in various sizes. Medical bags were much in evidence, either open on the tables, or at their feet as they prepared to submit their diagnostic opinions on the flower of Yorkshire's youth.

We were ordered to strip to the waist and passed from table to table, teeth chattering, as eyes, teeth, heart and lungs were speedily examined and our height and weight duly recorded. The procession of youth was a sorry sight as each of us attempted to retain a hold on sagging trousers with one hand, whilst clutching a bundle of discarded clothing with the other.

'Take this and go behind the screen' ordered a venerable white-haired M.D. kindly, as he handed me a tapered glass with the comment 'You can leave your clothing on the chair'. I tripped smartly behind the screen clearly thankful for the glass of hot milk that I thought I was about to be proffered. I remained standing there for some minutes wondering whether I was expected to pass through the nearby door — for, there was no sign of the anticipated beverage!

The impatient elderly medic suddenly peered anxiously around the screen. 'Have you done it?' he demanded. 'Done what Sir?' I stammered in reply. He looked in surprise at the empty glass in my hand. 'Oh, pee in the glass!' he said grunting, and promptly disappeared. I had never on any previous occasion been invited to do what the gentleman was now demanding, and felt that he might have been merely indulging in an unfortunate turn of phrase! At that moment, the next candidate joined me

behind the screen. He was somewhat small and ferret-like and obviously older than most of the intake. However, he quickly provided a dazzling display of what it was I was expected to do, and promptly disappeared behind the screen in the opposite direction. I was now quite intimidated by the proceedings and, but for the cold weather, it seemed unlikely that my own meagre performance could have taken place.

The final encounter of the morning was with a military gentleman of mature years, sporting a crown on his shoulder, a large moustache and a very florid complexion. 'Sit down Booth' he said without looking up from the mass of paperwork in front of him on the desk as I sat self-consciously clutching my discarded clothing. 'Oh for God's sake put your clothes on' he demanded somewhat irritably, the sidelong-glance at my skeleton-like torso having clearly upset his concentration.

'I have to decide which branch of the army you would be best suited to' said the major feelingly. 'Are you any relation to the Booth's gin people?' he enquired hopefully. He seemed disappointed with my negative reply. 'What would you like to serve in?' he enquired with pen poised. 'The RAF if I could Sir'. He turned purple. 'Dammit man, if they had wanted you for the airforce, you wouldn't have been here today,' he remonstrated heatedly. I countered quickly. 'I am sorry Sir, but you are the first person that has asked me about a choice'.

He returned his attention to the paperwork on the desk as I waited patiently for the next question, which in the circumstances I thought was rather badly phrased. 'Have you a father?' he demanded. I nodded, 'Yes I have Sir'. 'Has he been in the Forces?' 'He served four years in the last war Sir' I answered proudly. The Major reflected for a moment before replying. 'What Regiment was he?' He wasn't sir, he was in the Royal Engineers.' He looked up and almost hissed — 'Well isn't the Royal Engineers a Regiment?'. 'No Sir, not according to father.' 'I see' he said, (but it was clearly obvious he didn't!) 'And what does your father say the Royal Engineers are?' 'He says the Royal Engineers is the Senior Corps of the British Army Sir,' I added with relish.

'Damn it man! If they had wanted you for the airforce you wouldn't have been here today.'

The major reflected for a moment. 'Well done young man, most perceptive. Would you also like to serve in your father's old Corps?' he asked almost kindly. I nodded, and he proceeded to cross out, all but one of the five headings on his piece of paper. It was difficult trying to read them upside down without the effort looking obvious. It was R.A. something, but it was certainly not the Royal Engineers . . .

'Right, you may go' ordered the major, head down and still writing. He looked up as I started to leave. 'Well, what do you say?' he demanded. I looked nonplussed for a moment . . er . . 'What for sir?' 'You say thank you sir for the opportunity to serve my Country!' 'Thank you sir,' I muttered meekly, and stumbled out from the illustrious presence.

On the way back to Selby in the bus I found myself wondering why it was that my service in the Royal Observer Corps had appeared to count for so little in my attempt to join the Royal Air Force. For more than a year I had worn airforce uniform. I had an Air Ministry Identity Card and had even collected several salutes one rainy day in York when wearing my bulky 'Zeekee' coat!

As my 18th birthday passed and Christmas approached, I had a distinct feeling that my experiences in recent years had somehow been a preparation of what was to come. Had not Winston Churchill said something about a feeling of destiny, and, like him, I was something of a romantic. I also shared General Montgomery's aversion as far as smoking and alcohol were concerned, but for different reasons — I could not afford either on my Observer's pay of two pounds a week!

Destiny called one bleak mid-December morning in the shape of another small buff O.H.M.S. envelope that lay face downwards on the lino of the kitchen floor. Father was busy shovelling the snow off his precious bridge and mother had gone shopping, so neither were able to share in the magic of the moment.

My orders were to report to the Barracks at Richmond, Yorkshire not later than 23.59 hours of the 27th December, the army's way of saying you must be in by midnight. A one-way rail voucher was enclosed. The only thing that appeared to be missing was a card from the Minister of War wishing me a Merry Christmas and Happy New Year! Perhaps we would soon have a Minister of Peace? and, if he was half as efficient as his counterpart; there might be hope for the nations.

I left York station on the afternoon of the 27th December and had a reasonably comfortable journey as far as Darlington. Here it seemed the entire British Army was waiting on the platform for the next (and only) train to Catterick Camp and Richmond. The 'Catterick Flyer' was something of an institution. At that time the London and North Eastern Railway undoubtedly held the unofficial record for the greatest number of people ever to be carried in five non-corridor coaches. This was achieved with a high proportion of the passengers lying on the luggage racks, and underneath the seats.

The little tank engine evenually left Darlington station with its five coaches more than filled to capacity, each compartment resembling the interior of a sardine tin. Ours still retained its pre-war illustrations urging the travelling public to sample the delights of Scarborough and Bracing Skegness. There was a fine view of Richmond Castle with the caption 'See Richmond in the Spring!' and beneath, the inevitable picture of Mr. Chad peering over his wall and scrawled beneath 'Wot! about the bloody winter mate?'

When we reached Catterick, the major part of the British Army appeared to leave the train and those remaining enjoyed compressed, but almost comfortable standing room for the rest of the journey to Richmond. There were a great many other civilians in my compartment and their silence and downcast appearance led me to think that they were hardly relishing this belated call to Arms. The train reached the station and was just on the point of stopping when the brakes were fiercely applied and the occupants of the carriage ended up in a sprawling mass on top of each other. I am sure the driver's action was quite deliberate. Obviously he didn't like the army either!

We clambered from the train clutching our precious belongings and were herded together in the roadway outside the station by a highly vociferous band of army sergeants, each apparently trying to out-shout the other as they yelled our names and gestured wildly with their clip boards. In a remarkably short space of time we ended up in orderly groups and were marched off through the town and up a steep and slippery hill in the direction of the barracks.

We must have looked a sorry sight as we struggled up the snow covered road with a sergeant marching alongside each group urging us to get into step. Thank goodness the inhabitants of Richmond town were wisely by their firesides for they would have entertained the gravest doubts about the future of the army had they seen its latest batch of Conscripts.

Whatever else one might say about the British Army, it had a happy knack of getting its priorities right, for our first stop was the cook-house. Here we were presented with a tin mug, together with a knife, fork and spoon and two mess tins, the latter smelling strongly of 'Brasso'. In a matter of minutes something like two hundred youths were feeding heartily on a meal of bangers and mash from one mess tin, whilst the other contained a liberal helping of wizened prunes covered with a congealed yellow mass that passed for custard.

The task of carrying personal belongings, two mess tins full of food, and a large mug of steaming tea, all at one and the same time, demanded rather more than normal dexterity. This was not helped by one of the sergeants bawling 'If you drop your food, you won't get any more,' which of course a number of unfortunate entrants managed to do, and so went hungry to bed.

As the meal ended there was a sharp rap on one of the tables and the sergeant who had brought our 'shower' from the station addressed the assembly. He informed us that he was Sergeant Roberts and was the Senior Sergeant, whatever that was supposed to mean. 'You are now in the British Army, the finest body of fighting men in the world' announced Sergeant Roberts proudly 'and in the next six weeks you will be transformed from the 'orrible lot I see before me into a smart body of efficient and disciplined soldiers. Looking at you, God knows how I am going to achieve it, but achieve it I will, even if some of you die in the process'

The sergeant continued with his homily and we sat listening intently, the consternation and remorse clearly visible on our faces. 'You have already been divided into platoons' went on the sergeant and you will now be marched to your billets by your respective platoon sergeants. There you will select a bed and then you will be taken to fill your mattresses.

By great good fortune (although we did not think so at the time) we later discovered that the redoubtable Sergeant Roberts was to be our platoon sergeant. He was a small wiry man, possibly in his early forties with a string of medal ribbons, a ruddy outdoor complexion and horned rimmed spectacles, He proved to be both civilised and educated, a rare combination in a senior non-commissioned officer at that time. His favourite word was 'Gillo' which he had no doubt acquired as a professional soldier in India. He was the smartest sergeant I ever encountered in my army career and wore a battle dress that could have been tailor made by Saville Row. On parade he was a martinet, but off duty he was a most interesting and caring individual.

Sergeant Roberts marched us over to a large barn-like building with our mattress covers under our arms. It *was* a barn, and piled high with clean wheat straw! 'Right fill up your mattresses', ordered Sergeant Roberts as some of us gazed at him in astonishment. 'Don't you worry, it's the most comfortable bed you will ever sleep on' said the sergeant confidently. Then he added a word of warning. 'Don't put too much straw in or you will roll off in the night. On the other hand, too little will mean you will have the bed springs sticking in your arse, and that could be very uncomfortable!'

We were awakened promptly at 6 am the following morning by Sergeant Roberts marching briskly through the billet with the shout 'Wakey! Wakey! get your feet on the floor'. He rattled the rails of the beds with his stick as he passed, the occupants jumping heavenward like startled rabbits. Several mattresses had lost tie-tapes, their unfortunate owners having slept on the bedsprings, as a mass of straw had disgorged on the floor, turning the room into something that now looked like the advance preparations for a Nativity play.

'Make the best of today because this is the last time you will wear civilian clothes until the war is over' said the sergeant happily. We hastily began to dress and made a dash for the wash-rooms, for neither billets, nor the surrounding 'offices' were heated although I noticed that all the pipes had been lagged with the usual military thoroughness.

After breakfast, a young corporal, who appeared to have his own room tacked onto the end of our billet, showed us how we were to make up our beds with three of the blankets folded in a certain way and the fourth one folded around them. He explained that we were to have a kit inspection every Friday morning and he would show us later how our kit had to be displayed.

At 8.30 am we marched to the legendary Quartermaster's Store to receive our uniforms, whilst the remainder of the platoon accompanied the corporal to the Camp Barber for a 'trim' as the corporal put it. The group returned looking very dejected for most of their hair had

. . . to the Camp Barber for a 'trim' as the Corporal put it.

gone which is when the expression 'skin-head' must first have originated! Some of the more fastidious of the group had apparently attempted to bribe the barber 'not to take too much off' and the payments were willingly accepted although the end results were exactly the same!

By lunchtime the platoon were all clad in khaki battledress and looking very much like the winning entry for a Tramp's Ball. The military 'outfitters' had considerable difficulty with me. I stood well over six feet in my socks but weighed a mere 11 stone. The exasperated fitter made four attempts with different battle-dress blouses before turning to his sergeant in despair. 'Sergeant, this bloke's like a bloody beanpole; either the blouse is too short or you can wrap it round him like a shawl'.

Sergeant Roberts stood watching the proceedings with great interest clearly to ensure that his platoon were properly fitted out and, hearing the comment, took over the task from the exasperated soldier. 'This one will do' said Sergeant Roberts; 'Give him another one the same size', whereupon he thrust it into my kit-bag with the comment 'When I order those for the Camp Tailor to fall out, you fall out and bring your two battledress blouses with you.'

He wandered off down the line of partly clad soldiers, inspecting each in turn as we were deluged with socks, vests, underpants, shirts, a tie and beret, steel helmet, respirator, various sizes of pack complete with webbing, a belt, gas-cape, boots, gaiters and so on. Sergeant Roberts marched to the head of the line as his men signed for the various items of equipment, adding 'Look after your equipment. If you lose any of it you could end up in the Glass House!'

The Sergeant appeared satisfied with the arrangements. 'Right get "fell in" in three ranks', he shouted, the platoon looking like the recipients of a military jumble sale. Clutching our new possessions he marched us back to the billet. 'Right' said Sergeant Roberts, 'When I give the order Fall out! I want to see you all do a smart turn to the right and double smartly away to the billet. Those for the Camp Tailor I want back here with their gear in two minutes. Right, Platoon fall out.'

There was a rush for the barrack room to shouts of 'Gillo, Gillo' as Sergeant Roberts rattled the nearby railings with his stick. The visit to the Camp Tailor proved to be a remarkable experience, except that there appeared to be about six of them, all civilians. We watched in wonder as they cut, patched, stitched and sewed with an ability that would have turned a bespoke tailor green with envy — a sort of service while you wait, that was as speedy as it was professional.

Then it was back to the barrack room where we each received a large cardboard box and a regulation length of string from the corporal in which to pack our civilian clothing, now shortly to be posted back to our homes at the entire expense of His Majesty. The army certainly seemed to think of everything.

We spent the next two or three days 'square bashing' the army term for regulation drill, as Sergeant Roberts marched us back and forth across the barrack square, often demonstrating the various movements for us to emulate. At first it was difficult with the parade ground covered by marching troops, each platoon having to listen for the commands of its particular sergeant. Fortunately, Sergeant Roberts made use of a fairly high pitched voice in which to deliver his orders that we readily recognised, although sometimes the pitch was so high that the last part of the command didn't materialise at all.

Our Company Commander was a giant of a man, a certain Captain J. J. Taylor, Green Howards, who stood well over six feet in height and was built in proportion. His second in command was quite the reverse, a small, fresh-faced young lieutenant who couldn't have been much over five feet tall and was clearly in some difficulty when it came to keeping up with his Captain on ceremonial occasions.

On the morning of our first official parade before the mighty Captain Taylor, Sergeant Roberts was acting as Company Sergeant-Major and took charge of the proceedings, his corporal taking charge of our platoon.

We were all standing on the edge of the parade ground as Sergeant Roberts started to march towards its centre, his drill-stick firmly under his left arm. 'Markers!' squealed the sergeant and off half a dozen of the tallest

'Our company commander was a giant of a man.'

recruits marched to join him on the parade ground, myself included. 'Parade, on your markers Quick March!'
yelled Sergeant Roberts and the platoons set off at a brisk
pace for their respective markers and were soon standing
stiffly to attention in ragged lines three deep as the platoons awaited his next command. 'Parade, Right Dress'.
This order resulted in the platoon members looking to
their right with right arm raised and touching the shoulder of the man on their right. Meanwhile the 'marker'
looks down each line of soldiers in turn and 'dresses
them' so that the lines of soldiers are straight.

'Parade Eyes Front!' commanded Sergeant Roberts and
eyes swivelled to the front as the best part of two hundred arms descended with a noise like a thunderclap. The
parade were now well ordered and silent, apart from the
regulation tread of the platoon sergeants as they marched
to take up their respective position at the head of each
platoon.

Sergeant Roberts appeared pleased with the performance and after casting a reflective glance in the direction of the Guard Room, gave the order for the parade to
'Stand at Ease!'

At that moment I spotted Captain J. J. Taylor emerging
from the Guard room followed by his second in command. 'Parade Atten . . . shun' shouted Sergeant Roberts
as he executed a smart about turn and stood rigidly to
attention as Captain Taylor headed towards him, swing-
ing his stick in his right hand as he strode purposefully
across the parade ground, with the poor young lieutenant
almost on the point of breaking into a trot behind him.

The Captain halted in front of Sergeant Roberts, thrusting his stick smartly under his left arm as Sergeant Roberts saluted with the words 'C Company all present and
correct Sir!' The Captain returned the salute and com-
menced his inspection, walking along the lines of rigid
petrified soldiers, with the lieutenant, Sergeant Roberts
and the appropriate platoon sergeant all marching re-
spectfully in his wake. The mighty J. J. seemed satisfied
with what he saw. 'Excellent Sergeant Roberts, please
stand the men at Ease.' The Sergeant did as he was bid.
'Stand Easy, men', ordered the Captain. (This meant you

could move, cough, adjust your hat — but not move your feet).

For some ten minutes Captain Taylor addressed his new Company, standing with feet apart, his stick clasped behind his back. We were to complete six weeks primary training before being sent to join our regiments. During that time our fitness would be improved and we would be taught the use of Small Arms including the rifle, Sten-gun, Light machine gun (Bren) and the Piat anti-tank weapon. 'You will also throw a course of live-grenades', added the Captain as an afterthought, perhaps remembering the young recruit whose life had been saved by the prompt action of his sergeant a few weeks before. The lad had managed to pull the safety pin and then very inconveniently dropped the grenade in the throwing trench!

As we stood listening to the Captain, I couldn't help thinking what a remarkable transformation had taken place in the rag-tag and bobtail bunch of youngsters who had arrived at Richmond less than one week previously.

With the inspection over, we marched off the parade ground with Sergeant Roberts marching almost jauntily alongside his leading platoon, perhaps relishing the weeks ahead before it was time to send us off to war!